Here's what is remarkable about this book: Bob's passion for helping people see their suffering from God's perspective does not blind him to the fact that suffering still hurts. As a result, he weaves together a compassionate, Christ-centered resource that radically renews one's thinking about suffering while respecting the reality of it. I thank God for the clarity and comfort Bob brings to those who are overwhelmed by suffering.

Sam Hodges IV, *Executive Producer, Church Initiative*

How do you deal with suffering and despair, the times when life seems so overwhelming that you just want to give up? Bob Kellemen has the answers. If you are looking for tired clichés ("Just put on a happy face"), impersonal academic discourse, and worldly wisdom, then this is not the book for you. But if you want a thoroughly biblical and intensely honest examination of suffering from someone who has walked the path from "Hurt to hope in Christ," then *God's Healing for Life's Losses* is just the book for you. Dr. Kellemen provides a biblical theology of suffering that is also a practical guide to moving from grieving to growth, a journey on the road to hope and worshiping God. This is an essential book, not only for pastors and counselors, but also for anyone who is suffering and overwhelmed by grief and despair.

Ian Jones, *Ph.D., Professor of Psychology and Counseling, Southwestern Baptist Theological Seminary*

God's Healing for Life's Losses takes on traditional thoughts about grief and loss and turns them upside down. Dr. Kellemen takes us down to take us up as he develops a biblical theology of suffering and hope. There is a refreshing honesty about the pain of loss and the permission to be real with God and others as we embrace the mourning process together. For those of you who are hurting, I would recommend an unhurried reading with time to work through the grief and growth workbook at the end of each chapter. This book is biblical, personal, and healing. I highly recommend it.

Garrett Higbee, *Psy. D., President, Twelve Stones Ministries and Executive Director, Harvest Biblical Soul Care*

Without quick fixes or easy steps, Dr. Kellemen goes beyond the simple self-help so common to popular-level works offering counsel for pain. With a consideration of the message of the whole counsel of God and appeals to the likes of the Puritan's "losses and crosses," Luther's "two levels of suffering," C. S. Lewis' "megaphone" of pain, and Hugo's *Les Miserables*, he provides a Calvary-shaped lens through which pain, loss, and despair can be converted to satisfaction with the face of God in Christ.

Eric C. Redmond, *Senior Pastor of Reformation Alive Baptist Church, Temple Hills, Md., and Assistant Professor of Bible and Theology, Washington Bible College, Lanham, Md.*

Understanding the relationship between God and our life losses is a valuable tool in our spiritual growth. In this volume, Dr. Kellemen goes beyond merely helping people recover from their painful situations to a point where a deeper resource can be found. Weaving together biblical texts with suffering's varied and personal contexts, he directs the reader into the potential for growth that life's losses present. Whether one reads the book for oneself or to better help others, Kellemen's book is a practical resource for pastors, counselors, and anyone who has ever tried to help a friend who is hurting.

John A. Jelinek, *Th.D., Vice President and Dean, Moody Theological Seminary and Graduate School*

I just love Dr. Bob Kellemen's heart. He is committed and compassionate about helping people. In *God's Healing for Life's Losses,* he writes with a scriptural sensitivity that communicates clearly to all people of all races. Anyone facing suffering and dealing with grief will learn how to face his sorrows face-to-face with God. This book is real and raw, offering Christ's healing hope for life's hurts. I highly recommend it for individual or grief group work—it will help heal.

Pam Perry, *Ministry Marketing Solutions Inc., Chocolate Pages Network, Founder, Co-Author of* Synergy Energy

I picked up Dr. Kellemen's book expecting it to be another quick read on the subject of suffering. That wasn't the case. Instead, I found it to be a work deserving a special place in my library to reference again and again. It was eye-opening in that it revealed the deepest longing in my heart to understand God's purpose and plans for my own pain and grief. In a fallen and broken world this book is a welcome companion along life's journey.

Tracy Haney, *Producer, Moody Radio*

Reading *God's Healing for Life's Losses* is like walking a beach with a godly friend who knows where your path has been and where you hope your path will take you. Dr. Kellemen's book is a relevant, extremely helpful faith guide for those longing for healing from a past sorrow or preparing for life's inevitable pain.

Steve Dewitt, *Senior Pastor, Bethel Church, Crown Point, Ind.*

Bob Kellemen skillfully uses a conversational writing style to engage his readers as he provides them with a thorough biblical and practical way to grieve, thrive, and grow. Dr. Kellemen's book shows his tremendous spiritual insight and wisdom, based on God's Word. He confidently affirms that as Christians we are victors in Christ because we know the end of the story.

Elias Moitinho, *Ph.D., LPC, Assistant Professor of Psychology and Counseling, Southwestern Baptist Theological Seminary*

While grief and loss are common to all of us, the manner in which we actually process our experience is often unique and personal. C. S. Lewis once wrote, "God whispers in our pleasures, speaks in our conscious, but shouts in our pain." For some, the journey toward healing and restoration seems clear and straightforward. For others, the way is more uncertain and challenging. In *God's Healing for Life's Losses*, Dr. Kellemen skillfully describes the necessary tasks for each stage of the grief and recovery process. With relevant illustrations and God's Word illuminating the path, readers will receive encouragement and hope as they move from mourning to morning.

Eric T. Scalise, *Ph.D., LPC, Vice President for Professional Development, The American Association of Christian Counselors*

GriefShare Endorsement

We had the privilege of interviewing Dr. Robert Kellemen to be on the roster of experts who appear on the *GriefShare* videos, shown at the thousands of *GriefShare* support groups meeting weekly around the world. During the interview, we were deeply impressed with his wise and gentle counsel. Robert is genuine. He's knowledgeable. And he cares. Plus, he has personally experienced the pain of grief. As a young man, Robert survived the emotional upheaval of losing his father.

Just as countless *GriefShare* participants have benefited from his insights, you will too, as you read *God's Healing for Life's Losses*. You'll find that Robert has the unique ability to:

- Comfort you with biblical truth without trivializing your pain.
- Help you reinterpret your grief experiences in ways that make you more aware of God's active role in your healing.
- Help you discover how to experience deep healing and lasting peace in a world of suffering and pain.

As you face your own grief, perhaps you feel as if you can't go on. Or maybe you wonder why you should. Maybe you question whether God is still there, and if He is, why you're hurting so deeply.

If those are your feelings and questions, embrace *God's Healing for Life's Losses*. It's a treasure, filled with stunning and comforting words about God's perspective on grief. Best of all, it's written by Dr. Robert Kellemen, a man who can guide you on each step of the journey from mourning to joy.

Steve Grissom
Founder, GriefShare
Christ-centered, Grief Support Groups
www.griefshare.org

ROBERT W. KELLEMEN, PH.D.

GOD'S HEALING
for LIFE'S LOSSES

How to Find Hope
When You're Hurting

bmhbooks.com
P.O. Box 544
Winona Lake, IN
46590

God's Healing for Life's Losses
Copyright © 2010 by Robert W. Kellemen

ISBN: 978-0-88469-270-6
RELIGION / Christian Life / Counseling and Recovery

Published by BMH Books
P.O. Box 544, Winona Lake, IN 46590
www.bmhbooks.com

The personal identities of individuals described in this book have been disguised to protect their privacy.

Unless otherwise noted, Scripture quotations are from *The Holy Bible: New International Version.* Copyright © 1973, 1978, 1984 by International Bible Society. Used by permission of Zondervan Publishing House. All rights reserved.

Scripture quotations noted KJV are from *The Holy Bible: King James Version.*

Scripture quotations noted NASB are from the *New American Standard Bible®*, Copyright © 1960, 1962, 1963, 1968, 1971, 1972, 1973, 1975, 1977, 1995 by The Lockman Foundation. Used by permission. www.Lockman.org

Scripture quotations noted *The Message* are from *The Message: The Bible in Contemporary Language.* Copyright © 2002 by Eugene H. Peterson. Used by permission of NavPress. All rights reserved.

Kellemen, Robert W.
God's healing for life's losses: how to find hope when you're hurting/Robert W. Kellemen

Printed in the United States of America
7th printing 2018

ACKNOWLEDGMENTS

To my dear friends who model biblical grieving with hope.

To them, and to all who cling to Christ, God the Father says:

"Fear not, for I have redeemed you;
I have summoned you by name;
you are mine.

When you pass through the waters,
I will be with you;
and when you pass through the rivers,
they will not sweep over you.
When you walk through the fire,
you will not be burned;
the flames will not set you ablaze.

For I am the LORD, your God,
the Holy One of Israel,
your Savior"
(Isaiah 43:1-3a).

You don't have to go through grief alone.

GriefShare is a safe place where you'll meet others who are facing the same confusing emotions and tough decisions as you. Participate in a GriefShare group and you'll benefit from:

- Helpful ideas on how to recover from grief
- Video interviews with Christian grief recovery experts
- Video testimonies of those who've healed from grief
- Small group discussion
- A comforting daily Bible study program

GriefShare groups are meeting all over the world. To find one near you, visit **GriefShare.org** or call **800-395-5755.**

Your journey from mourning to joy
www.griefshare.org

Dr. Robert Kellemen,
GriefShare Expert
GriefShare features more than

40 top Christian grief recovery experts— including Dr. Robert Kellemen, author of *God's Healing for Life's Losses.*

FOREWORD

I have had the privilege of serving as a pastor of the same congregation for more than twenty years. On the one hand, God has graciously given numerous opportunities to share in the joys and blessings of my parishioners and friends. There have been many births, weddings, spiritual victories, and occasions for laughter and love. Countless days have been filled with far more sweetness than I would have ever imagined.

But the parallel truth is that I have seen firsthand how often men and women suffer. Job losses. Shocking diagnoses. Children gone astray. Abuse. And the caskets—oh, so many caskets. I knew the Bible predicted this would occur, but it's different when it happens to members of your church family, your own family, your friends, and to you.

Of course, you know that as well. I have never met a person who has not suffered in some way. That explains why Jesus' family is instructed to "weep with those who weep" (Romans 12:15 NASB). Life this side of heaven is anything but trouble-free.

That is why I am so glad Dr. Bob Kellemen wrote *God's Healing for Life's Losses*. You cannot choose whether you will face suffering or not, but you can decide where you will turn for help. Here are three reasons why I heartily and joyfully encourage you to read carefully what Bob has written.

It courageously faces the hard questions. You are probably fed up with pat answers and pious platitudes. Plastic smiles do not work, not when you are suffering. Bob writes with the seasoned wisdom of a winsome counselor who has spent many hours compassionately listening to people whose hearts are breaking.

It skillfully takes you to God's Word. Listening is wonderful and powerful, but it is seldom enough. Bob is a careful student of the Bible.

He believes that the living God has direction and answers for every hurting person who will humbly come to Him (Matthew 11:28-30). I went to college and seminary with Bob—I know that he is a diligent and accomplished student and scholar. Yet this book does not read like a distant theological treatise. It is more like a wise conversation with a mature spiritual friend.

It passionately points you to the Savior. The Bible is less like an encyclopedia and more like a novel. Bob's goal is not to give us a few verses that we simply memorize and recite when times get rough. He is inviting us to use suffering as an opportunity to grow more in love with the One who suffered supremely for us. That is why there is hope for life's losses.

I look forward to the day this project goes from the manuscript I currently have in my hand to a book I can read and give to others. My church family needs it. My counselees need it. I need it. And, if you're suffering a loss or helping someone who is grieving, then you need it.

One more thing. Bob and I grew up a few miles from one another in Gary, Indiana. I have known him since we were boys running around the neighborhood. I can say this without reservation—Bob is the real thing. He cares deeply about people who are suffering. That is one of his God-given passions. Let this book be a gift to you, from a dear and trusted friend.

Dr. Steve Viars, *Senior Pastor, Faith Baptist Church, Lafayette, Indiana*

CONTENTS

INTRODUCTION
There Is Hope

———◆———

JESUS PROMISES THAT LIFE WILL BE FILLED WITH LOSSES.

I know. That's not exactly the promise you were hoping for. At least it's honest.

In John 16:33, Jesus guarantees that we will suffer. "I have told you these things, so that in me you may have peace. In this world you *will* have *trouble*" (emphasis added).

LIFE'S LOSSES

One word says it all: *trouble*. "You're gonna' get squashed!" is a fair paraphrase. Hemmed in, harassed, and distressed. Oppressed, vexed, and afflicted.

Trouble communicates both external and internal suffering. External suffering: illness, poverty, criticism, abandonment, and death. Internal suffering: fear, anxiety, anguish, depression, and grief.

The Bible repeatedly recites Jesus' not-so-wanted guarantee. Consider just a few samplers:

- Genesis 45:1-11; Genesis 50:20
- Deuteronomy 8:1-10
- Psalm 13; Psalm 42; Psalm 73; Psalm 77; Psalm 88
- Job: The whole book!
- Jeremiah and Lamentations
- John 9:1-3
- Romans 5:3-5; Romans 8:17-39
- 2 Corinthians 1:3-11; 2 Corinthians 4:1-18
- 2 Timothy 3:12
- Hebrews 4:14-16; Hebrews 10-12
- James 1:2-18
- 1 Peter 1:3-9; 1 Peter 2:11-25.

From passages like these, we learn that *we are not alone*. In this life, we *all* suffer.

Life is filled with losses.

MY PROMISE TO YOU:
REMAINING REAL AND RAW

I suspect that I'm preaching to the choir. You're reading this book because the raw reality of life's losses haunts you everywhere everyday.

I also imagine that you've grown weary of Christian books that pretend. They're far too Pollyannaish for you. You're tired of Christian counselors and well-meaning spiritual friends who dispense too much "happiness all the time, wonderful peace of mind."

Frank Lake vividly describes what happens when we fail to face suffering honestly and refuse to engage sufferers passionately.

> The pastoral counselor, in spite of himself, finds himself tittering out his usual jocular reassuring prescriptions, minimizing the problem, and thumping in optimism or the need for further effort. He has the ingrained professional habit of filling every unforgiving minute with sixty seconds' worth of good advice.[1]

There has to be a better way, don't you think?

Here's my promise to you. I'm not giving you pabulum. No trite platitudes. No false promises. No pretending.

We'll remain real and raw like the Puritans who labeled suffering "losses and crosses." We'll go deep into the abyss of affliction like J. I. Packer who understands the gravity of grinding affliction.

> There is an umbrella-word that we use to cover the countless variety of situations that have this character, namely *suffering*. Suffering . . . may conveniently be defined as *getting what you do not want while wanting what you do not get*. This definition covers all forms of loss, hurt, pain, grief, and weakness—all experiences of rejection, injustice, disappointment, discouragement, frustration, and being the butt of others' hatred, ridicule, cruelty, callousness, anger, and ill-treatment—plus all exposure to foul, sickening, and nightmarish things that make you want to scream, run, or even die. . . . *Ease is for heaven, not earth*. Life on earth is fundamentally out of shape and out of order by reason of sin. . . . So strains, pains, disappointments, traumas, and frustrations of all sorts await us in the future, just as they have overtaken us already in the past.[2]

How do we face such losses and crosses? How do we handle life's strains and pains? Our purpose is to answer such candid and confusing questions honestly and biblically.

GOD'S HEALING: CREATIVE SUFFERING

Of course, if all we do is talk about life's losses, then that too fails to tell the whole story. We need to be able to deal with life's losses *in the context of* God's healing.

Jesus did. "I have told you these things, so that *in me* you may have *peace*. In this world you will have trouble. But *take heart*! I have *overcome the world*" (John 16:33, emphasis added).

Peace. With one word Jesus quiets the quest of our soul. We thirst for peace—shalom, wholeness, stillness, rest, healing.

Take heart. Hope. Come alive again.

That's what you long for. I know it is, because it's what I want.

We live in a fallen world and it often falls on us. When it does, when the weight of the world crushes us, squeezes the life out of us, we need hope. New life. A resuscitated heart. A resurrected life.

*We live in a fallen world
and it often falls on us.*

Brilliantly, the apostle Paul deals simultaneously with grieving *and* hoping. Do not "grieve like the rest of men, who have no hope" (1 Thessalonians 4:13). Paul, who offers people the Scriptures and his own soul (1 Thessalonians 2:8), skillfully ministers to sufferers.

To blend losses and healing, grieving and hoping, requires *creative suffering.* Frank Lake powerfully depicts the process. "There is no human experience which cannot be put on the anvil of a lively relationship with God and man, and battered into a meaningful shape."[3]

Notice what the anvil is—a lively relationship with God and God's people. Notice the process—battering. Notice the result—meaning, purpose. What cannot be removed, God makes creatively bearable.

Another individual, this one intimately acquainted with grief, also pictures creative suffering. British hostage Terry Waite spent 1,460 days in solitary confinement in his prison cell in Beirut. Reflecting on his savage mistreatment and his constant struggle to maintain his faith, he reveals:

> I have been determined in captivity, and still am determined, to convert this experience into something that will be useful and good for other people. I think that's the way to approach suffering. It seems to me that Christianity doesn't in any way lessen suffering. What it does is enable you to take it, to face it, to work through it and eventually convert it.[4]

Creative suffering doesn't simply accept suffering; through the *Cross it creatively converts* it. Our passion is to learn together how to grieve, but not as those who have no hope.

HOW TO FIND HOPE WHEN YOU'RE HURTING

So, how do you find hope when you're hurting? It's certainly not through any "quick fix." Nor are there any "secrets" or any "easy steps."

Let's be honest. Growth through grieving is an arduous journey, much like the journey of Much-Afraid, the lead character in Hannah Hurnard's dramatic allegory, *Hinds' Feet on High Places*.

Tired of valley living, but terrified to trek the high places alone, Much-Afraid asks Shepherd for companions on her journey. Encouraged by his pledge that fellow travelers would soon join her, she starts alone, anticipating the arrival of her partners. When they appear, she's horrified. Shepherd introduces them.

> They are good teachers; indeed, I have few better. As for their names, I will tell you them in your own language, and later you will learn what they are called in their own tongue. "This," said he, motioning toward the first of the silent figures, "is named Sorrow. And the other is her twin sister, Suffering."[5]

Poor Much-Afraid! Her cheeks blanched and she trembled from head to toe.

> "I can't go with them," she gasped. "I can't! I can't! I can't! O my Lord Shepherd, why do you do this to me? How can I travel in their company? It is more than I can bear . . . Couldn't you have given me Joy and Peace to go with me, to strengthen and encourage me and help me on the difficult way? I never thought you would do this to me!" And she burst into tears.[6]

A strange look passed over Shepherd's face.

> "Joy and Peace. Are those the companions you would choose for yourself? You remember your promise, to accept the helpers that I would give, because you believed that I would choose the very best possible guides for you. Will you still trust me, Much-Afraid?"[7]

Don't misunderstand. Fear of suffering is normal. Grief is necessary. Shepherd is not denying these authentic life responses.

So just what is Shepherd saying?

Trust me.

Trust is vital because suffering is inevitable. How do we find hope when we're hurting? Through trust.

Where do we find God's healing for life's losses? In Christ. With Christ.

IT'S A PERSONAL JOURNEY –
WITH A PERSONAL GOD

Moving through hurt to hope is a journey—a personal journey. Finding God's healing for life's losses is a trek—a messy trail with far more detours than we would ever wish.

That's why I'm not promising you eight easy steps. However, as we journey together, I will offer you eight biblical markers on your personal healing journey. As you begin exploring these trail markers for life's trials, you'll experience the ups and the downs, the hills and the valleys, the zigs and the zags.

View these markers as your personal suffering *GPS: God's Positioning System,* derived from God's Word. Nothing ever written can compare with the honesty and reality of the Word of God. It is totally sufficient to light our path. It is utterly profound in its capacity to resonate with our experiences.

The eight biblical markers empower us not to evade suffering, but to face suffering face-to-face with God.

The various "stages" we'll explore in the grief journey provide compass points in God's process for hurting and hoping. They empower us not to evade suffering, but to *face suffering face-to-face with God.*

When tragedy occurs, we enter a crisis of faith. We either move toward God or away from God. We'll probe how to move in the direction of *finding God* in the midst of our suffering.

The end in sight is not quick answers through easy steps. Our goal is deep healing through a personal journey—with God, in Christ. He never lets you walk alone.

OUR JOURNEY TOGETHER

Through *God's Healing for Life's Losses*, I invite you to walk with God and God's people. At the end of chapters two through nine, you'll find two built-in "Grief and Growth Workbooks." In the first, you'll be able to trace your journey, and in the second, you'll be able to journal about your healing process.

While you can read and apply *God's Healing for Life's Losses* alone, I've also designed it for group use. Consider gathering with some other spiritual friends to share your progress along your journey. At the very least, invite one other friend to be "Jesus with skin on" for you.

Grief tempts us to walk alone. Fight that temptation. Walk with God and His people as you journey on the healing path.

CHAPTER ONE
The Way of Suffering

———•———

CONSIDER THE CONTRAST BETWEEN THE FIRST FIVE WORDS AND the last five words of Genesis. "In the beginning God created" (Genesis 1:1). "In a coffin in Egypt" (Genesis 50:26).

The Bible begins with life. Within two chapters it introduces death. In fact, all but four chapters of the Bible (Genesis 1-2 and Revelation 21-22) address our slavery to death—"in a coffin in Egypt."

GOD'S PRIMER ON HURTING AND HOPING

Given that 1,185 out of the 1,189 chapters in the Bible cover suffering and death, you would think that we'd have a clear-cut "theology of suffering." Unfortunately we don't.

While theologians cover all sorts of theological topics, such as "Christology" for the study of Christ, and "anthropology" for the study of human beings, you won't actually find a "sufferology"—a *biblical theology of suffering*—in theology text books.

Biblical Sufferology

Levels of Suffering: Causes of Grief

Level One Suffering: External Suffering
- Circumstances: What Happens *to* Us—Relational Separation
- Theological Reality: Our World Is Fallen and It Often Falls on Us

Level Two Suffering: Internal Suffering
- Condemnation: What Happens *in* Us—Spiritual Depression
- Personal Reality: Our World Is a Mess and It Messes with Our Minds

Sustaining in Suffering: Stages of Hurt
"It's Normal to Hurt and Necessary to Grieve"

Stage	*Typical Grief Response*	*Biblical Grief Response*
Stage One	Denial/Isolation	Candor: Honesty with Myself
Stage Two	Anger/Resentment	Complaint: Honesty with God
Stage Three	Bargaining/Works	Cry: Asking God for Help
Stage Four	Depression/Alienation	Comfort: Receiving God's Help

Healing in Suffering: Stages of Hope
"It's Possible to Hope and Supernatural to Grow"

Stage	*Typical Acceptance Response*	*Biblical Growth Response*
Stage Five	Regrouping	Waiting: Trusting with Faith
Stage Six	Deadening	Wailing: Groaning with Hope
Stage Seven	Despairing/Doubting	Weaving: Perceiving with Grace
Stage Eight	Digging Cisterns	Worshiping: Engaging with Love

It's well past time for a change. *God's Healing for Life's Losses* is your personal overview of 1,189 chapters (you can't skip the first two or the last two chapters if you want hope!) in the Bible and what they teach us about *biblical sufferology*—about how to find hope when you're hurting.

What do we find in God's primer on hurting and hoping?

- Levels of Suffering: Causes of Grief
- Sustaining in Suffering: Stages of Hurt
- Healing in Suffering: Stages of Hope

We'll apply the levels of suffering to our lives in this chapter. We'll explore and apply the stages of hurt in chapters two through five, and we'll discover and apply the stages of hope in chapters six through nine.

LEVELS OF SUFFERING: WHY DOES IT HURT SO MUCH?

Martin Luther was an astute student of suffering, both personally and theologically. He found that we always experience suffering as a trial of faith. He experienced and identified two levels of faith trials:

- *Level One Suffering*: What happens *to* us and around us—what we are facing. This is the external "stuff" of life to which we respond internally. I lose a job, my child is ill, I face criticism, my spouse leaves me, a loved one dies. Level one suffering involves our situations and our circumstances—what happens to us.

- *Level Two Suffering*: What happens *in* us—how we face what we are facing. Level two suffering is the suffering of the mind that gives rise to fear and doubt as we reflect on our external suffering. It is what happens in us as we face our circumstances. Do we doubt, fear, and run away from God? Or do we trust, cling, and face our suffering face-to-face with God? How do we respond internally to our external situations?

LEVEL ONE SUFFERING: WHAT HAPPENS TO US—RELATIONAL SEPARATION

Suffering is so dreadful because suffering is *death*. All suffering is the dying, separating, and severing of relationships. Eternal death means to perish, to be cut off, lost, dead, separated from God forever (John 3:16-17). Eternal death/separation is the paradigm of all our losses.

Ultimately, we experience all suffering as death. Whether it's the little death of a flat tire, or the bigger death of a broken engagement, or the grand death that ends our earthly life, we each face daily casket experiences. These casket journeys are not the way things are supposed to be. We were not meant to end up in a coffin in Egypt. Death is an intruder.

Walter Wangerin, in his healing book, *Mourning into Dancing*, expresses more insight into death than any mortician.

> Death doesn't wait till the ends of our lives to meet us and to make an end. Instead, we die a hundred times before we die; and all the little endings on the way are like a slowly growing echo of the final *Bang* before that bang takes place.[1]

Because reality is relational, death is separation. All deaths, all caskets, are the same—the sundering of relationships.

In suffering, God is not getting back at you;
He is getting you back to Himself.

So why would Shepherd send Suffering and Sorrow to guide us? What are they supposed to teach us? Throughout *Mourning into Dancing*, Wangerin explains that *suffering and death are meant to teach us our need again*. Paul learned from the same lesson plan.

> We do not want you to be uninformed, brothers, about the hardships we suffered in the province of Asia. We were under great pressure, far beyond our ability to endure, so that we despaired even of life. Indeed, in our hearts we felt the sentence of death. But this happened that we might not rely on ourselves but on God, who raises the dead (2 Corinthians 1:8-9).

In suffering, God is not getting back at you; He is getting you back to Himself. "The actual experience of dying persuades the little god that he is finite after all."[2] When Paul felt the sentence of death, he understood that his only hope was the dead-raising God.

Opening Our Hands to God

Suffering opens our hands to God. It was Augustine who declared, "God wants to give us something, but cannot, because our hands are full—there is nowhere for Him to put it."

Moses taught the same truth in the passage Jesus quoted during His temptation. Why does God allow us to endure desert wanderings? According to Deuteronomy 8 and Matthew 4, it is to humble us, teaching us how desperately needy we are.

Our greatest need is eternal life and we experience eternal life in intimacy with God (John 17:1-3). Therefore, suffering reveals God's extraordinary love. Without suffering we would forget God and our need for Him (Deuteronomy 8:6-18).

Suffering is grace. It was grace that barred Adam and Eve from the tree of life, lest they live forever, immortal immoral beings, never having to face their need for God. "Perhaps we suffer so inordinately," Peter Kreeft reminds us, "because God loves us so inordinately and is taming us."[3] God loves us too much to allow us to forget our neediness.

God makes therapeutic use of our suffering. Luther taught that suffering creates in the child of God a *delicious despair*. Suffering is God's putrid-tasting medicine of choice, resulting in delicious healing.

Healing medicine for what? For our ultimate sickness—the arrogance that we do not need God.

Suffering causes us to groan for home and to live in hope. The author of Hebrews, surveying the landscape of Old Testament journeys, shows us the way home.

> All these people were still living by faith when they died. They did not receive the things promised; they only saw them and welcomed them from a distance. And they admitted that they were aliens and strangers on earth. People who say such things show that they are looking for a country of their own. If they had been thinking of the country they had left, they would have had opportunity to return. Instead, they were longing for a better country—a heavenly one. Therefore God is not ashamed to be called their God, for he has prepared a city for them (Hebrews 11:13-16).

God refuses to allow us to get too comfy here. Instead, He allows suffering—daily casket processionals—*to blacken our sun so we cry out to His Son.* Suffering reminds us that we're not home yet.

At least, that's God's intent. Satan plots an altogether different strategy. We learn about his scheme in level two suffering.

LEVEL TWO SUFFERING: WHAT HAPPENS IN US—SPIRITUAL DEPRESSION

The *theological* reality of suffering teaches that our world is fallen and it often falls on us. The *personal* reality of suffering tutors us in the truth that *our world is a mess and it messes with our minds.* Suffering is not only what happens *to* us, it is also, and more importantly, what happens *in* us.

Our world is a mess and it messes with our minds.

All suffering and mourning amount to a sense of death, divorce, aloneness, and forsakenness. The doubts that we endure while in the casket of suffering lead to a potential hemorrhage in our relationship to God, others, and self so that we end up feeling:

- Spiritual Abandonment: "I feel forsaken."
- Social Betrayal: "I feel betrayed."
- Self Contempt: "I feel ashamed."

Spiritual Abandonment: "I Feel Forsaken"

In spiritual abandonment, I see God as my enemy (Job 3:1-26; 6:4; 10:1-3; Psalm 13; 88; Jeremiah 20:7-18; Lamentations 3:1-20; 5:20). Luther called this aspect of level two suffering "spiritual depression." It's the trial of faith produced when I reflect on and interpret my suffering with reason unaided by faith.

It results in a terrified conscience in which I perceive that God is against me, and in the sense of ultimate terror that God may have forsaken me. *The presence of suffering can result in the absence of faith.*

I call it "spiritual separation anxiety"—the terror of a sense of abandonment. Satan incites this terror when he whispers, "Life is bad. God controls life. God must be bad, too. How can you trust His heart? He has left you all alone. Again."

Spiritual depression and spiritual separation anxiety are the results of our *internal* interpretations of *external* events. They are satanic temptations to doubt God, spiritual terrors, restlessness, despair, pangs, panic, desolation, and desperation. The absence of faith in God in the presence of external suffering leads to a terrified conscience which perceives God to be angry and evil instead of loving and good.

Jeremiah felt and expressed such condemnation and rejection. "Why do you always forget us? Why do you forsake us so long?" (Lamentations 5:20). In Jeremiah 20:7, his language is even stronger, making us squeamish. "O Lord, you deceived me, and I was deceived; you overpowered me and prevailed."

Heman, considered one of the wisest believers ever (1 Kings 4:31), pens the "Psalm of the Dark Night of the Soul" (Psalm 88) in which his concluding line summarizes his spiritual struggle. "You have taken my companions and loved ones from me; the darkness is my closest friend" (verse 18).

If you're honest, if I'm honest, we admit that we've felt what Heman felt. We've thought what Jeremiah thought.

Social Betrayal: "I Feel Betrayed"

As if excruciating spiritual abandonment were not enough, level two suffering continues with social betrayal. In social betrayal we're bombarded by paradoxical realities. "Extra! Extra! Read All About It! 'Bob learns that you can't live without trusting. And Bob finds that you can't live without betrayal.'"

Trust *and* betrayal.

Joseph faced it everywhere from everyone. Betrayed by his brothers, by slave traders, by Potiphar's wife, by Potiphar, and by the baker.

David, too, knew betrayal. He speaks for all of us when he describes the wracking torment of broken trust.

If an enemy were insulting me, I could endure it; if a foe were raising himself against me, I could hide from him. But it is you, a man like myself, *my companion, my close friend*, with whom I once enjoyed sweet fellowship as we walked with the throng at the house of God (Psalm 55:12-14, emphasis added).

Who has not said similar words? Which of us has not shed similar tears?

Self Contempt: "I Feel Ashamed"

To spiritual abandonment and social betrayal we add self contempt. "If God and others reject me," we surmise, "then I must be unworthy of their friendship. Something must be wrong with *me*. I am not only at fault. I am faulty."

Job loathed his very life (Job 10:1). He lost all hope for himself and his future. "My days have passed, my plans are shattered, and so are the desires of my heart" (Job 17:11). He felt stripped of honor, torn down, hope uprooted (Job 19:9-10).

STAGES OF HURT AND STAGES OF HOPE

What are we to do when we're assaulted outside and in? How are we supposed to survive, much less thrive, when we're overwhelmed by circumstances and feeling condemned by God, our friends, and our own soul?

How do we move from suffering to creative suffering? How do we suffer face-to-face with God rather than turning our backs on God during suffering? How does God expect us to find *hope when we're hurting*?

THE WORLD'S WAY: IS THAT ALL THERE IS?

We have two basic options. We can turn to the world's way. Or we can follow the way of God's Word.

Students of human grief have developed various models that track typical grief responses. Swiss-born psychiatrist Elizabeth Kubler-Ross, in *On Death and Dying*, popularized a five-stage model of grieving based upon her research into how terminally ill persons respond to the news of their terminal illness. Her five stages have since been used worldwide to describe all grief responses.

A Researched-Based Model of the Grief Process

- *Denial*: This is the shock reaction. "It can't be true." "No, not me." We refuse to believe what happened.
- *Anger*: Resentment grows. "Why me?" "Why my child?" "This isn't fair!" We direct blame toward God, others, and ourselves. We feel agitated, irritated, moody, and on edge.
- *Bargaining*: We try to make a deal, insisting that things be the way they used to be. "God, if You heal my little girl, then I'll never drink again." We call a temporary truce with God.
- *Depression*: Now we say, "Yes, me." The courage to admit our loss brings sadness (which can be healthy mourning and grieving) and/or hopelessness (which is unhealthy mourning and grieving).
- *Acceptance*: Now we face our loss calmly. It is a time of silent reflection and regrouping. "Life has to go on. How? What do I do now?"[4]

Understanding the World's Limitations

These proposed stages in the grief process seek to track *typical grief responses*. However, they do not attempt to assess whether this is what is *best to occur*. Nor could they assess, simply through scientific research, whether these responses correspond to *God's process for hurting (grieving) and hoping (growing)*.

We must understand something about research in a fallen world. At best, it *describes* what typically occurs. It cannot, with assurance and authority, *prescribe* what should occur. Research attempts to understand human nature are thwarted by the fallenness of our nature and of our world.

As Dallas Willard explains:

Secular psychology is not in an "at-best" set of circumstances. The question of who we are and what we are here for is not an easy one, of course. For those who must rely upon a strictly secular viewpoint for insight, such questions are especially tough. Why? Because we do in fact live in a world in ruins. We do not exist now in the element for which we were designed. So in light of that truth, it's essentially impossible to determine our nature by observation alone, because we are only seen in a perpetually unnatural position.[5]

Understanding these research limitations, and believing in the sufficiency of Scripture, we will focus on a revelation-based model. We will address and assess the typical five stages of grieving. However, we want to move beyond them.

The biblical approach to grieving and growing identifies eight scriptural "stages" in our responses to life's losses. God's way equips us to move through hurt to hope in Christ—from grieving to growing.

The first four stages involve what we call *sustaining in suffering*, which we will explore in chapters two through five. The second four stages relate to *healing in suffering*, which we will examine in chapters six through nine.

Please remember that these "stages" are a relational process, not sequential steps. Grieving and growing are not a neat, nice package. It isn't a tidy procedure.

Grieving and growing are messy because life is messy. Moving through hurt to hope is a two-steps-forward, one-step-backward endeavor. We don't "conquer a stage" and never return to it.

Rather than picturing a linear, step-by-step route, imagine a three dimensional maze with many possible paths, frequent detours, backtracking, and even the ability to reside in more than one "stage" at the same time.

However, positive movement is possible. In fact, it is promised. You *can* find God's healing for your losses. You *can* find hope in your hurt.

Whatever your grieving experience has been like up to this point, don't quit. Don't give up.

Join the journey. Experience the biblical reality that *it's normal to hurt and necessary to grieve*. Learn how to move from denial to personal honesty (candor), from anger to honesty with God (complaint), from bargaining to asking God for help (crying out), and from depression to receiving God's help (comfort).

Stay on the path. Experience the biblical reality that *it's possible to hope and supernatural to grow*. Learn how to move from regrouping to trusting with faith (waiting on God), from deadening to groaning with hope (wailing to God), from despair to perceiving with grace (weaving in God's truth), and from digging cisterns to engaging with love (worshiping God and ministering to others).

God truly does provide you with everything you need for life and godliness. Through the Word of God, the Spirit of God, and the people of God, you have all you need for your healing journey.

Your journey begins with "candor"—being honest with yourself. Chapter two will be your guide, your map, directing you from the world's way of denial, to the Word's way of facing life face-to-face with God.

CHAPTER TWO
Candor: Blessed Are Those Who Mourn

SOMETIMES WE THINK OF CHARACTERS FROM THE BIBLE AS "SUPER Saints." Like Superman, we imagine they have a huge *S* scripted across their chest. And we assume that, like Superman, they are invincible, invulnerable.

SUSTAINING: "IT'S NORMAL TO HURT AND NECESSARY TO GRIEVE"

It's not true. They're flesh and blood just like us. The kryptonite of suffering and grief weakens them just like it does us. Truly, it is normal to hurt.

That's why the apostle Paul was so candid; it's why he wanted his friends to be aware of the hardships he was suffering. He shared with them that he was under great pressure, far beyond his ability to endure, so that he despaired even of life. In fact, he felt the sentence of death (2 Corinthians 1:8-9).

You've been there, done that, haven't you? I know I have.

Some of us get there and we feel like we're all alone, isolated, friendless.

Some of us get to that point and we're ready to escape, to retreat, to raise the white flag of surrender.

SUSTAINING IN SUFFERING:
DRAWING A LINE IN THE SAND OF RETREAT

Caring Christians throughout church history have recognized the tendencies toward isolation, escape, and retreat. To combat them, they have practiced *sustaining*.

In sustaining, we refuse to allow one another to suffer alone. We come alongside one another to grieve together. We understand that *shared sorrow is endurable sorrow*.

I picture sustaining with the rather macabre image of *climbing in the casket*. When friends despair of life and feel the sentence of death, we enter their casket experience with them.

Although I can't be physically present with you now, and I don't know the exact casket you're currently enduring, I want you to know that *you are not alone*. And I want you to know that it's normal to hurt and necessary to grieve.

I pray that the words you read and the applications you make will help you to begin to draw a line in the sand of retreat. Hope deferred makes the heart sick, weak. Deferred hope tempts us to give up in helplessness.

But there is help. There is hope.

We find help and hope as we journey together through the four biblical stages that define the grief process. Together we'll climb in the casket of candor, complaint, cry, and comfort. We'll mourn together, for blessed are those who mourn, for they shall be comforted.

SUSTAINING IN SUFFERING: STAGES OF HURT
"IT'S NORMAL TO HURT AND NECESSARY TO GRIEVE"

Stage	*Typical Grief Response*	*Biblical Grief Response*
Stage One	Denial/Isolation	Candor: Honesty with Myself
Stage Two	Anger/Resentment	Complaint: Honesty with God
Stage Three	Bargaining/Works	Cry: Asking God for Help
Stage Four	Depression/Alienation	Comfort: Receiving God's Help

CANDOR: MOVING FROM DENIAL TO HONESTY WITH MYSELF

The first four stages in biblical grieving compare and contrast with the first four stages in the typical response to suffering.

1. *Stage One: Candor—Honesty with Myself*
    We move from denial and isolation to candor: honesty with ourselves.
2. *Stage Two: Complaint—Honesty with God*
    We move from anger and resentment to complaint: honesty with God.
3. *Stage Three: Cry—Asking for God's Help*
    We move from bargaining and works to crying out to God: asking God for help.
4. *Stage Four: Comfort—Receiving God's Help*
    We move from depression and alienation to comfort: receiving God's help.

DENIAL: SHOCK AND AWE

Research informs us that people's typical first response to loss is *denial*. When suffering first hits; when we first hear the news of the unexpected death of a loved one; when we're told that we've been fired; we respond with shock. We can't believe it. Life seems unreal.

I experienced this when I was 10 years old. It was December and I was coming home from Riddle's Pond where Billy Trapp and I had been playing hockey. My Mom pulled up, rolled down the window, and said, *"Get in the car. Grandpa died."*

My response?

"You're kidding."

As if my Mom would kid about something like that. I was in shock. In denial.

Denial is a common initial grief response. I believe that this initial response can be a grace of God, allowing our bodies and physical brains to catch up, to adjust. However, after a necessary period of time, long-term denial is counter-productive. More than that, it is counter to faith, because *true faith faces all of life.*

I once worked with a pastor who was struggling to move past denial. His wife had died while giving birth to their second child. He denied the reality for months. He continued preaching, continued ministering. He never grieved, never wept. He put on a happy face.

Behind the scenes, he was a mess. He imagined that he saw and heard his deceased wife. He was near the point of a total emotional and spiritual collapse, largely because he could not move out of the stage of denial and into the stage of candor.

CANDOR: HONESTY WITH MYSELF

Courageous truth telling to myself about life in which I come face-to-face with the reality of my external and internal suffering.

CANDOR: TELLING YOURSELF THE TRUTH

The world has its way of grieving. But, when our fallen world falls on us, when suffering crushes us, we need much more than *research*. We need *revelation*—we need God's inspired truth about how to grieve as those who have *hope*.

God's Word offers us profound practical wisdom for moving from denial to *candor*. What exactly is biblical candor? Candor is *courageous truth telling to myself about life in which I come face-to-face with the reality of my external and internal suffering.* In candor, I admit what is happening to me and I feel what is going on inside me.

I had to move from denial to candor after the death of my father on my 21st birthday. In fact, it was not until my 22nd birthday that the process truly began. I had been handling my loss like a good Bible college graduate and seminary student—I was pretending!

On my 22nd birthday, one year to the day after my father's death, I went for a long walk around the outskirts of the seminary campus. That day I started facing my loss of my Dad. The reality that I would never know him in an adult-to-adult relationship. The fact that my future children would never know their grandfather.

As I faced some of those *external loses*, the tears came. Then I began to face some of the *internal crosses*—what was happening in me. I felt like a loner. Fatherless. Orphaned. Unprotected. On my own. The tears flowed. The process of candor began. The floodgate of emotions erupted. I was being honest with myself.

BIBLICAL CANDOR SAMPLERS: FEARLESSLY FACING THE FACTS

But was it biblical? Does God really allow and even invite His children to be brutally honest about life? Can we support candor biblically?

David practices candor in Psalm 42:3-5.

My tears have been my food day and night, while men say to me all day long, "Where is your God?" These things I remember as I pour out my soul: how I used to go with the multitude, leading the procession to the house of God, with shouts of joy and thanksgiving among the festive throng. Why are you downcast, O my soul? Why so disturbed within me?

Notice that David is honest about his *external* suffering. He describes his *losses*—the loss of fellowship, leadership, and worship. He also is candid about his *internal* suffering. He depicts his *crosses*—accurately labeling his soul as downcast and disturbed within him.

Job consistently models candor throughout his response to his losses: "What I feared has come upon me; what I dreaded has happened to me. I have no peace, no quietness; I have no rest, but only turmoil" (Job 3:25-26). Again we witness brutal frankness both about external losses and internal crosses.

We could profitably examine the accounts of other biblical characters who practiced candor—Jeremiah, Solomon, Asaph (Psalm 73), Heman (Psalm 88), Jesus, Paul, and so many more. They all convey the same inspired message: it's normal to hurt and necessary to grieve.

The apostle Paul does not tell us not to grieve; he tells us not to grieve *without hope* (1 Thessalonians 4:13). He chooses a Greek word meaning to feel sorrow, distress, and grief, and to experience pain, heaviness, and inner affliction.

Paul is teaching that grief is the grace of recovery because mourning slows us down to face life. No grieving; no healing. Know grieving; know healing.

No grieving; no healing.
Know grieving; know healing.

The only person who can truly dare to grieve, bear to grieve, is the person with a future hope that things will eventually be better. When we trust God's good heart, then we trust Him no matter what. We need not pretend. We can face and embrace the mysteries of life.

ON THE ROAD TO HOPE

Candor or denial. The choice is a turning point. It is a line drawn in the sand of life, a hurdle to confront.

Faith crosses the line. Trust leaps the hurdle. We face reality and embrace truth, sad as it is. If facing suffering is wrestling face-to-face with God, then candor is our decision to step on the mat. Will you?

RELATING TRUTH TO LIFE:
YOUR CANDOR GRIEF AND GROWTH WORKBOOK

Grieving is not just about reading. It's about relating—relating *God's* truth to *your* life. Because we're all different and because the grief journey is filled with twists and turns, we end every chapter with different types of "grief and growth exercises."

Pick and choose. Don't feel that you have to do each part of each exercise in each chapter. Piece together your own grief and growth workout routine that resonates with and fits you.

In this chapter, I've designed some grief and growth work exercises to help *you* to move from *denial to candor*—brutal, frank honesty with yourself about your losses and crosses. They will help you to trace your candor *journey*—what your path has been like so far and how you can continue to move forward. And they'll help you to launch your candor *journal*—putting words (whether written or thought) to your grief.

YOUR CANDOR JOURNEY

1. True faith faces all of life. Where would you put yourself on a scale of 1-10, with 1 being total denial and 10 being facing all of life—internal and external suffering?

2. In past experiences of suffering, how did you begin to move from denial to candor?

3. As you reflect on what you are grieving over, what are your external losses—what has happened to you and around you?

   a. What is missing?

   b.   What has been robbed from your life?

   c.   What are you grieving over the most?

4. As you ponder your suffering, what are your inner crosses—your feelings about your loss and the trials of your faith?

   a.   What feelings do you associate with these losses?

   b.   Have you ever faced anything like this before? How did you feel then?

   c.   How has your suffering impacted your relationship with and your attitude toward God?

   d.   How has your suffering impacted your faith, hope, and love?

5. Find a trusted, safe friend and take the "baby steps" of sharing with him or her some of your candor.

YOUR CANDOR JOURNAL

1. Read Matthew 27:45-46 and Luke 22:39-45. How can Jesus' candor with Himself, His disciples, and with God influence you?

2. Read 2 Corinthians 1:8-9 and 2 Corinthians 4:7-12. Pen your own candid story of your suffering and grieving.

3. Read Psalm 13, and/or Psalm 88. Write your own candid psalm, expressing your feelings.

4. Read Lamentations 3:1-20 to probe what it is like to feel abandoned by God. How does Jeremiah's experience compare to yours?

5. Read Job 3:1-26; 7:1-10; and 10:1-22 to sense Job's despair and dread. Have you been there? How so? How did you respond?

6. According to Job 17:11-16 and Proverbs 13:12, how do dashed dreams impact us? How have they impacted you?

YOUR JOURNEY CONTINUES

I know. For some it's like, *"This can't end here, right?"*
Good question. Fair question.
No. Biblical grieving does not end with candor. It *begins* with candor. Where it heads next is our topic for chapter three: *Complaint: A Lament for Your Loss.*

CHAPTER THREE
Complaint: A Lament for Your Loss

———◆———

MANY PEOPLE FIND THAT THE HARDEST PART OF THE GRIEF journey is simply getting started. Stepping on the trail by facing the pain and the hurt can be terrifying. All manner of questions arise.

"What will I feel? Will I be able to handle whatever I feel? What if my thoughts consume me and my feelings overwhelm me? Will anyone understand? Will anyone join me? Is it worth it? What's the point?"

Moving from denial to candor—honesty with yourself—requires courage. It takes time. Effort. Energy. Resilience.

Candor is worth it. Denial changes nothing. Denial only prolongs the inevitable. Pretending doesn't change the facts and can't alter reality.

If you haven't already, consider stepping on the path. Perhaps it would be best if you returned to chapter two to jump start your candor journey.

COMPLAINT: MOVING FROM DESTRUCTIVE ANGER TO CONSTRUCTIVE HONESTY WITH GOD

If you've started your healing journey, then you're walking down the path from denial to candor. You're telling yourself the truth. You're facing the facts.

In a Christian approach to grieving, we can't stop here. God is our ultimate reality. We can't and shouldn't try to escape facing our grief face-to-face with God. To our candid honesty with ourselves we must add honesty with God. We need to lament. We need to move from destructive anger *at* God to constructive complaint *to* God.

FACING DESTRUCTIVE ANGER

Anger is the typical "second stage" in the world's grieving journey. Forsaking denial, the truth sinks in. Something bad, horrific has occurred. We've lost something or someone dear to us.

Our loss frustrates our desires and blocks our goals. It ticks us off. We're mad. We want to lash out. At life. At the world. At . . . God.

This is where grief gets very confusing for the committed Christian. We love God; we know He loves us. We know God is good; we know life has now turned bad. So we want to know, sometimes we want to scream it, *"How could a good God allow such evil and suffering?"*

But dare we ask? Do we dare verbalize our complaint, our lament to God?

The Scriptures are clear—*God invites lament, complaint.* The Bible repeatedly illustrates believers responding to God's invitation with honest words that would make many a modern Christian shudder.

I know what you're thinking. "Didn't God judge the Israelites for complaining?"

There are different words and a distinct context between the sinful complaint of the Israelites in Numbers and the godly complaint/lament of Job, the psalmists, Jeremiah, and many others. Biblical complaint complains *to* God about the fallen world. Ungodly complaint complains *about* God and accuses Him of lacking goodness, holiness, and wisdom.

We must remember that Satan is the master masquerader (2 Corinthians 11:13-15). His counterfeit for biblical complaint is unhealthy, destructive anger. Satan wants us to substitute cursing for complaint.

Job's wife fell into Satan's snare when she urged Job to "Curse God and die!" She encouraged him to give up on God, on himself, and on life.

Cursing God demeans God. It sees Him as a lightweight, as an arid desert and a land of great darkness (Jeremiah 2:5, 19, 29, 31). Cursing separates. Complaint connects. Complaint draws us toward God; hatred and anger push us away from God.

BIBLICAL COMPLAINT: TELLING GOD THE TRUTH

What then is complaint? In candor we're honest with ourselves; in complaint we're honest to God. Complaint is *vulnerable frankness about life to God in which I express my pain and confusion over how a good God allows evil and suffering.*

———◆———

COMPLAINT: HONESTY WITH GOD

Vulnerable frankness about life to God in which I express my pain and confusion over how a good God allows evil and suffering.

———◆———

We needlessly react against the word "complaint." "Christians can't complain!" we insist. Yet numerically, there are more psalms of complaint and lament than psalms of praise and thanksgiving.

Complaints are faith-based acts of persistent trust. They are one of the many moods of faith. Psalm 91's exuberant trust is one faith mood while Psalm 88's dark despair is another faith mood. A mood of faith trusts God enough to bring everything about us to Him. In complaint we hide nothing from God because we trust His good heart and because we know He knows our hearts.

MY PERSONAL COMPLAINT/LAMENT JOURNEY

In the weeks and months after my 22nd birthday, I engaged in passionate complaint. What made my struggle with my father's death even more difficult was my lack of assurance that my father was a believer. I had witnessed to him, prayed for him, and he even began attending church with me. Yet even on his deathbed, he made no verbal commitment of faith in Christ.

So I shared with God. I complained to God. I told God, "What's the use? Why did I pray, witness, and share? Why should I ever pray again? Why should I ever try again, trust again?"

I shared my confusion and my doubt with God. "Why does everyone else's parent accept Christ in a glorious deathbed conversion? Why can't I have assurance of my Dad's presence with You?"

Were my expressions of complaint biblical? Can complaint be biblically supported? Does God truly prize complaint?

BIBLICAL COMPLAINT SAMPLERS:
WITH CHRIST IN THE SCHOOL OF SUFFERING

According to Psalm 62:8, if we truly trust God, then we'll share everything with God. "Trust in him at all times, O people; pour out your hearts to him, for God is our refuge."

Complaint is an act of truth-telling faith, not unfaith. Complaint is a rehearsal of the bad allowed by the Good.

The biblical genre of complaint expresses frankness about the reality of life that seems inconsistent with the character of God. Complaint is an act of truth-telling faith, not unfaith. Complaint is a rehearsal of the bad allowed by the Good.

When we complain, we live in the real world honestly, refusing to ignore what is occurring. Complaint is our expression of our radical trust in God's reliability in the midst of real life.

Psalm 73 is a prime example of complaint. Asaph begins, "Surely God is good to Israel" (v. 1). He then continues with a litany of apparent evidence to the contrary, such as the prosperity of the wicked and the suffering of the godly (vv. 2-15). When he tries to make sense of all this, it's oppressive to him (v. 16). He then verbalizes to God the fact that his heart is grieved and his spirit embittered (v. 21).

His lament, his complaint, drew him nearer to God. It did not push him away from God. "Yet I am always with you; you hold me by my right hand" (v. 23). He concludes, "But as for me, it is good to be near God. I have made the Sovereign LORD my refuge" (v. 28).

It was Asaph's intense relationship *with* God that enlightened him to the goodness *of* God even during the badness of life. "Till I entered the sanctuary of God; then I understood their final destiny. . . . As a dream when one awakes, so when you arise, O LORD, you will despise them as a fantasy" (vv. 17, 20). Spiritual friendship *with* God results in 20/20 spiritual vision *from* God.

---

*Spiritual friendship with God
results in 20/20 spiritual vision from God.*

Asaph illustrates that in complaint we come to God with a sense of abandonment and confusion (Isaiah 49:14; Jeremiah 20:7; Lamentations 5:20). We then exercise a courageous, yet humble cross-examination. Not a cross-examination of God, but a cross-examination and a refuting of earth-bound reality with spiritual reality.

That's exactly what occurs in Jeremiah 20:7, Lamentations 5:20, and Psalm 88:18. In all three passages, it appears *by reason alone* that life is bad *and so is God*. Yet in each passage, God responds positively to a believer's rehearsal of life's inconsistencies.

In Job 3, and much of Job for that matter, Job forcefully and even violently expresses his complaint.

> What's the point of life when it doesn't make sense, when God blocks all the roads to meaning? Instead of bread I get groans for my supper, then leave the table and vomit my anguish. The

worst of my fears has come true, what I've dreaded most has happened. My repose is shattered, my peace destroyed. No rest for me, ever—death has invaded life (Job 3:23-26, *The Message*).

In Job 42:7-8, God honors Job's complaint saying that Job spoke right of life and right of God. God prizes complaint and rejects all deceiving denial and simplistic closure, preferring candid complexity.

To deny or diminish suffering is to refuse arrogantly to be humbled. It is to reject dependence upon God. Moses chastises God's people in Deuteronomy 8:1-10 for forgetting their past suffering. God wants us to make use of our suffering, to remember our suffering, to admit our need for Him in our suffering, and to rehearse our suffering (external and internal) before Him.

ON THE ROAD TO HOPE

Destructive anger or constructive complaint/lament? We find ourselves at another major choice point. Will we be disappointed with God or disappointed without God? We can either complain with and to God, or we can complain without and about God.

If facing suffering is wrestling face-to-face with God, then complaint is our decision to grapple with God about life hand-to-hand, eye-to-eye. Will you?

RELATING TRUTH TO LIFE:
COMPLAINT/LAMENT GRIEF AND GROWTH WORKBOOK

Remember, everyone's grief journey is unique. So, when using these complaint grief and growth work exercises, pick and choose. Don't feel that you have to do each part of each exercise. Piece together your own complaint/lament workout routine that resonates with and fits you.

In this chapter, I've designed your grief and growth work to help *you* to move from *destructive anger to constructive complaint/lament*—bold honesty with God about your losses and crosses. I've created them to help you to trace your complaint *journey*—what your path has been like and how you can continue to move forward. And I've shaped them to help you to cultivate your complaint *journal*—putting words (whether written or thought) to your grief.

YOUR COMPLAINT/LAMENT JOURNEY

1. Biblical complaint/lament trusts God's good heart enough to bring everything about us to Him. Where would you put yourself on a scale of 1-10, with 1 being anger that pushes God away because you doubt His good heart, and 10 being complaint/lament that invites God in because you trust His good heart?

2. In past suffering, how did you begin to move from destructive anger to biblical complaint/lament?

3. How would you compare your response to your suffering to Job's? Jeremiah's? Jacob's? David's? Paul's? Jesus in the Garden?

4. Perhaps you've begun to face your losses and crosses. Where does Christ fit into your picture? What are you doing with Christ in your suffering? Have you been able to share your heart with God? If so, what have you said? If not, what would you like to say?

5. Find a trusted, safe friend and take the step of sharing with him or her some of your complaint/lament.

YOUR COMPLAINT/LAMENT JOURNAL

1. What do you think the Bible teaches about expressing anger and disappointment to God? What passages could you ponder to discover how God's people have talked to God when they experienced loss?

2. Psalm 62:8 indicates that when we trust God we openly pour out our whole heart to Him, trusting in Him as our refuge. Pour out your heart to God—everything and anything—in prayer, or in a journal, or in your own lament psalm.

3. Read Psalm 88—The Psalm of the Dark Night of the Soul.

    a. What does Psalm 88 suggest about expressing your anger, disappointment, or complaint to God?

    b. If you were to pen your own Psalm 88, what would it sound like? What would you write?

4. How would you respond if Satan sent someone to you to say, "Curse God and die"?

5. Read Lamentations 3:1-20. How does Jeremiah's experience compare to yours? To what extent do his words express your feelings?

6. Read Job 3:1-26; 7:1-10, and 10:1-22. Have you been there? How so? Pen your own Job-like expression of lament to God.

Your Journey Continues

Many people who courageously embark on the journey of complaint and lament end up feeling, *"Now you've opened a real can of worms! Now I have all these feelings. This emotional mess. What in the world am I supposed to do now?"*

I won't lie to you. I promised to be real and raw. Candor and complaint leave us vulnerable.

If we follow the way of the world, then we deal with our sense of defenselessness through "bargaining"—trying to manipulate God into being good to us by doing good works. We try to regain control by controlling God!

In chapter four we take a different route. It's marked *Cry*, as in crying out to God. Vulnerable, we cry out to our Comforter. Left defenseless, we cry out to God our Rock and Defender. Let the journey toward God and with God continue.

CHAPTER FOUR
Cry: I Surrender All

———

AS I'M WRITING, I'M PICTURING YOU—MY READERS, MY SPIRITUAL friends. I imagine some of you tentatively sticking the tip of a single toe in the water of candor and complaint. Others, I envision jumping in cannonball style.

CRY: MOVING FROM BARGAINING TO CRYING OUT TO GOD

We're all different. We all process our grief in different ways at a different pace. But one thing is for sure; when we honestly face our hurt, it can feel overwhelming. And when we're overwhelmed with life, regardless of our personalities, we basically have two choices.

We can try to manage life on our own. We can play *Let's Make a Deal* with God through works-based bargaining.

Or, we can surrender control of our life to God. We can quit playing games with God and we can cry out, *I Surrender All!*

BARGAINING/WORKS: A TIT-FOR-TAT GOD

The typical third stage of the grief journey moves from denial to anger and then to bargaining and works. The dying people that Elizabeth Kubler-Ross interviewed entered into spoken and unspoken bargains with God. They believed God would reward them for their good behavior and grant them special favors.

They reasoned, "If I'm good, then God will be good to me." Their unstated theology said, "Good things happen to good people." So, of course, they told themselves, "God will stop the bad things that are happening to me if He sees what a good person I am and what good I can do."

Job's miserable counselors followed the identical mindset. Their God was a tit-for-tat God. "If you do bad, then God does bad back to you. If you do good, then God does good to you."

CRY: ASKING GOD FOR HELP

A faith-based plea for mobilization in which I humbly ask God for help based upon my admission that I can't survive without Him.

We can summarize their entire counsel to Job as, "Behave, be good, do right, be righteous, and God will treat you right." That is why they wrongly assumed and cruelly asserted that Job's suffering was all a direct result of Job's sinning.

Frank Lake has strong words for such harsh counselors then and now. Speaking of innocent sufferers and one-dimensional counselors, Lake explains:

> These passive evils, which are not of the soul's own making, are not accessible to a pastoral care which can talk only in terms of the forgiveness of sins. Such sufferers are usually not insensitive to their status as sinners. They have sought God's forgiveness.

But like Job, they complain of the comforters whose one-track minds have considered only the seriousness of sin, and not the gravity of grinding affliction.[1]

Such false counsel leads to bargaining that knows nothing of grace. It is all works, self-effort, and self-sufficiency. Bargaining attempts to control and manipulate God. That's why it is so vital to move from bargaining and works to cry—crying out to God for help.

CRYING OUT TO GOD: OPEN PALMS AND PLEADING EYES

What do I mean by "cry"? What is it?

Cry is *a faith-based plea for mobilization in which I humbly ask God for help, based upon my admission that I can't survive without Him.* Crying is reaching up with open palms and pleading eyes in the midst of darkness and doubt.

MY PERSONAL CRYING OUT TO GOD JOURNEY

Throughout the 22nd year of my life, as I grieved my father's death, I cried out to God for help. Up to this point in my Christian life, without knowing it, I had believed the lie that I could control life through my good behavior. As my scaffolding collapsed, I could work harder at being even better, or I could give up on God, or I could surrender to God. I chose surrender.

> God, I'm confused. I'm scared. Everything I trusted in is gone. I used to think that if I only prayed hard enough and worked long enough, that eventually everything I longed for would come true in this life. But now I know that's a lie. So what is true? What have You really promised? What can I count on? I can't count on myself. Father, I want to count on You. Please don't let me down. Rescue me. Help me. Save me.

BIBLICAL CRYING OUT TO GOD SAMPLERS: THE GOD WHO COLLECTS OUR TEARS

Did God hear my cries? Were my cries biblical? Can we find biblical support for cry as a scriptural stage of grief?

Psalm 56:8 (NASB) teaches that we pray our tears and God collects them in His bottle. Psalm 72:12 assures us, "For he will deliver the needy who cry out" ("when he crieth" KJV).

Psalm 34 reminds us, "The righteous cry out, and the LORD hears them; he delivers them from all their troubles. The LORD is close to the brokenhearted and saves those who are crushed in spirit" (vv. 17-18).

I learned the significance of these particular verses from a counselee whose husband had left her for another man. Yes, another man. She clung to the truth, and taught me the truth, that God's good heart goes out, especially, to the humble needy. She practiced biblical crying out to God—the hopeful, trusting plea for God to mobilize Himself on her behalf.

Crying out to God is a testimony that God is responsive, while all false gods and idols are non-responsive (1 Samuel 12:20-24). When we cry out, we entreat God to help because expressed neediness compels God's very character to act. God acts on voiced pain. He is not a deaf and dumb idol.

Crying empties us so there is more room in us for God. David wept until he had no strength left, but then he found strength in the LORD (1 Samuel 30:6). His cry, his confession of neediness, summoned God into action—supportive action.

---

*Crying empties us
so there is more room in us for God.*

Suffering is God's primary way of uprooting our self-reliance and complacency. He uses suffering to gain our attention. Suffering is a slap in the face, the shock of icy water, a bloodied nose meant to snatch our attention. Crying out to God is our admission that God has our attention, that God has *us*.

ON THE ROAD TO HOPE

You've come to another choice point. Bargaining with God or crying out to God? Your choices are works, self-sufficiency, control, and manipulation, or grace, God-sufficiency, surrender, and humility.

If facing suffering is wrestling face-to-face with God, then crying out to God is crying "Uncle." Or, to use the current image—"tapping out," admitting defeat. We say, "I'm pinned. I'm helpless. Life has defeated me. In self, I lose. With and in Christ, I win by giving in and asking for help." Which are you choosing?

RELATING TRUTH TO LIFE: YOUR CRYING OUT TO GOD GRIEF AND GROWTH WORKBOOK

As with candor and complaint, your crying out to God journey is unique to you. When you use these crying out to God grief and growth exercises, don't feel that you have to do each part of each one. Create your own crying out workout routine that is best for you.

In this chapter, I've designed your grief and growth work to help *you* to move from *works-based bargaining to grace-based crying out to God*—humbly admitting to God that you can't survive your sorrow without Him. My prayer is that the following exercises will help you trace your crying out to God *journey*—what your path has been like so far and how you can continue to move forward. And I pray that the exercises will help you nurture your crying out to God *journal*—putting words (whether written or thought) to your grief.

YOUR CRYING OUT TO GOD JOURNEY

1. In crying out to God, you admit to yourself your insufficiency, and you verbalize to God His all-sufficiency. Where would you put yourself on a scale of 1-10, with 1 being self-sufficient, bargaining, works, trying to control and manage your grief on your own, and with 10 being God-sufficiency, surrendering, trusting, humbly asking God for help?

2. In your past suffering, how did you begin to move from bargaining and self-sufficiency to admitting to God that you can't survive without Him?

3. As you reflect on your response to your loss, do you see any evidence of bargaining and works—of trying to get God to relent and to be good to you by your being good? If so, where do you think this mindset comes from? How could you begin to shift from works to crying out to God?

4. Crying out to God is like saying, "Hello, my name is Bob and I am in desperate need of help!" What would it be like for you to cry out to God, "Hello, my name is _____ and I desperately need you, God"?

5. Picture yourself, and perhaps do this now, reaching up to God, open palms, pleading eyes, asking God to mobilize His mercy on your behalf.

6. Find a trusted, safe friend and take the step of admitting to her or him that you can't handle your grief on your own. Let that friend be "Jesus with skin on" for you.

YOUR CRYING OUT TO GOD JOURNAL

1. Why do you think it is so hard for us to admit to God that we can't survive without Christ?

2. As in Psalm 13, how could your situation cause you to cry out to God for help, love, strength, joy, peace, and deliverance?

3. If you were to write a Psalm 72 or 73 (psalms of crying out to God), how would it sound? What would you write?

4. Do you believe that God collects your tears (Psalm 56:8)? How can you apply this verse to your pain?

5. Psalm 34:17-18 teaches that God's good heart goes out especially to the humble needy. How could you apply this truth in your life now?

6. Read the following verses: Psalm 56:8; Psalm 72:12; Psalm 34:17-18. Write your own personalized paraphrase of their message for your grieving.

7. C. S. Lewis wrote, "God whispers to us in our pleasures . . . but shouts in our pains: it is His megaphone to rouse a deaf world."[2] What message is God shouting to you in your pain? Does He have your attention? Your dependence?

8. Crying empties us so there is more room in us for God. David wept until he had no strength left, but then he found strength in the LORD (1 Samuel 30:6). Invite God in; make room for Him today in your grief.

YOUR JOURNEY CONTINUES

So you cry out to God. Now what? Is it one-sided—you call out and God is inattentive, silent, and inactive? Or, does God listen, speak, and act?

If we do not find ourselves face-to-face with the God of all comfort, then it would not be surprising that we experience the fourth stage in the world's grieving process—depression. It is a sure prescription for depression if we cry "I'm helpless!" and then no one comes to our rescue.

When we cry out to God, exactly what does the Bible promise? What was Jesus saying to your grieving heart when He guaranteed that in Him you could have peace? When Jesus promised not to leave you as an orphan, but to send another Comforter, what sort of comfort was He pledging?

In chapter five we explore the path marked *Comfort*. We probe what it is like to experience the presence of God in the presence of suffering. I'll join you on the other side.

CHAPTER FIVE
Comfort: God Comes

———•———

FACING SUFFERING REQUIRES US TO WRESTLE FACE-TO-FACE WITH God. In stage one—*candor*—we make the courageous decision to step on the mat. In stage two—*complaint*—we grapple hand-to-hand with God about life. In stage three—*cry*—we cry "Uncle." We "tap out" and admit that life has pinned us, and we desperately need God's help. We've fallen and we can't get up.

COMFORT: MOVING FROM DEPRESSION TO RECEIVING GOD'S HELP

High school and collegiate wrestling matches have three periods. If the score is tied at that point, you enter overtime. Consider stage four of the grieving process—*comfort*—your intense, sudden-death overtime period with God.

In cry, we ask for God's help. In comfort, we receive God's help. In comfort, the God we cry out to, comes. However, God does not necessarily come in the way we might expect. For He comes to comfort us with His crippling touch that plants the seed for future healing.

DEPRESSION/ALIENATION: GRIEF WITHOUT HOPE

Imagine a person's location on the grief journey after the first three typical stages. Denial has given way to anger, which has given way to bargaining and works.

*If God allowed work to work,
no one would ever surrender to God.*

If God allowed work to work, no one would ever surrender to God. So He thwarts our attempts to manipulate Him, to make life work on our own, and to change our circumstances.

Thwarted by God, if we refuse to cry out to Him, the typical fourth stage of grief happens—depression. It is a depression filled with hopelessness because of our chosen separation from God. We accept the reality of our loss, but only from an earthly perspective. We see no higher plan.

This stage of depression and alienation reminds me of the chilling opening scene in the musical *Les Miserables*. Hundreds of prisoners are chanting, "Look down, look down, don't look them in the eyes." They're filled with shame.

Then one prisoner attempts to break free from his emotional prison by singing that there are people who love him and are waiting for him when he's released. The guards and even the other prisoners heap more shame upon him. One cries, "Sweet Jesus doesn't care!" Others sing, "You'll always be a slave, you're standing in your grave."

That's hopelessness. That's the fourth stage of grief without Christ. Or, as Paul says it in 1 Thessalonians 4:13, it is grieving without hope.

In stage four, our journey leads us either to depression because of alienation and separation from God and others, or to finding comfort through communion with God and connection with God's people. For those who do not turn to Christ, the grief process moves from denial to anger, to bargaining/works, and then to depression. For those who cling to Christ, for those who grieve with hope, the journey moves from candor, to complaint/lament, to crying out to God, and then to comfort.

COMFORT: SURVIVING SCARS

What is comfort? Before we offer a definition, let's enjoy a little history lesson. Remember that historic sustaining draws a line in the sand of retreat. Horrible things happen to us. We're charging headlong away from the life we once dreamed of. We're ready to give up and give in.

Sustaining steps in to say, "Yes, you do have a wound. You will have a scar. But it is neither fatal nor final. Don't quit. You can make it. You can survive."

COMFORT: RECEIVING GOD'S HELP

Experiences the presence of God in the presence of suffering—a presence that empowers me to survive scars and plants the seed of hope that I will yet thrive.

It's within this context of surviving scars that I'm using the word "comfort." Originally, comfort meant *co-fortitude*—being fortified by the strength of another. Being *en-couraged*—having courage poured into you from an outside source. That outside source is Christ and the Body of Christ. In this life, your scar may not go away, but neither will His. He understands. He cares. He's there.

Now we can define comfort. Comfort *experiences the presence of God in the presence of suffering—a presence that empowers me to survive scars and plants the seed of hope that I will yet thrive.* At the end of sustaining, I'm not necessarily thriving. More likely, I'm limping, but at least I'm no longer retreating.

For me, comfort reflected itself in my decision not to give up on God and not to give up on ministry. Here I was in seminary, preparing for ministry, and secretly doubting God—doubting His goodness, His trustworthiness, His ability, or at least His desire to protect me and care for me. As comfort came, I came face-to-face with God. We had some wild talks. We had some fierce wrestling matches.

God won. I surrendered. I was still confused about the details of life, but committed to the Author of Life. More than that, I surrendered to Him *and* was dependent upon Him. My attitude was like Peter's when Jesus asked His disciples, "Will you, too, leave me?" Remember Peter's reply? "To whom else could we go? You alone have the Words of life" (John 6:67, 68).

I was surviving again, surviving though scarred. I was not and never again would be that same naïve young Christian who assumed that if I prayed and worked hard enough, God would grant me my every expectation. My faith was not a naïve faith; it was now a deeper faith—a faith that could walk in the dark.

BIBLICAL COMFORT SAMPLERS: WRESTLING WITH GOD

Did my experience of comfort reflect a biblical process? Can we biblically support comfort, as we've pictured it, as a legitimate stage in the grieving/healing process?

Jacob's wrestling match with God certainly illustrates it. Recall the context. Jacob is terrified that his brother Esau will kill him. In self-sufficiency, Jacob plans and plots ways to manipulate Esau into forgiving him.

Then, at night Jacob encounters God. He wrestles God throughout the night until God overpowers Jacob by dislocating his hip. In response, "Jacob called the place Peniel, saying, 'It is because I saw God face-to-face, and yet my life was spared'" (Genesis 32:30). Jacob shows us that tenacious wrestling with God results in painful yet profitable comfort through communion.

As the sun rose, Jacob was limping. He looks up and there's Esau. Jacob limps up to Esau and, with the pain of his dislocated hip, bows down to the ground seven times. Imagine the excruciating pain. Each time he bows down, pain shoots through his crippled body.

Then Jacob receives from Esau an embrace instead of a dagger. He faced his fear, still wounded and scarred, but surviving. God humbled Jacob, weakened him, and in the process strengthened him.

What is illustrated in Jacob's life is taught in Asaph's story. According to Psalm 73:21-28, suffering is an opportunity for God to divulge more of Himself and to release more of His strength. When Asaph's heart was grieved, and his spirit embittered, God brought him to his senses. Listen to his prayer. "My flesh and my heart may fail, but God is the strength of my heart and my portion forever" (Psalm 73:26).

In grieving we say with Asaph, "My flesh may be scarred, my heart may be scared, but with God I can survive—forever."

Thus faith perceives that God feels our pain, joins us in our pain, and even shares our pain. In fact, faith believes that, "in all their distress he too was distressed" (Isaiah 63:9). His sharing of our sorrow makes our sorrow endurable.

Faith does not demand the removal of suffering;
faith desires endurance in suffering.

Faith does not demand the removal of suffering; faith desires endurance in suffering, temptation, and persecution (1 Corinthians 10:13). Faith understands that what can't be cured, can be endured. Faith delights in weakness, because when we are weak, then God is strong, and we are strong in Him (2 Corinthians 12:9-10).

Grieving is a normal response to loss. However, God does not abandon us in our dark, dank casket. God, who is Light, shines His light of comfort into our hurting hearts.

Comfort develops through communion with Christ *and* through connection to the Body of Christ. The great soul caregivers of the past called human comfort *compassionate commiseration.* Think about those words. *Co-passion*: sharing in one another's passion and pathos. *Co-misery*: sharing misery with one another. It is because we experience suffering as separation, that shared sorrow (compassionate commiseration) is so vital.

On the Road to Hope

The grieving journey is filled with choice points, forks in the road. In stage one, we choose either denial or candor, in stage two either anger or complaint, in stage three either bargaining/works or crying out to God, and in stage four either depression or comfort.

As we wrestle face-to-face with God in our suffering, we experience God's crippling touch. As the great Soul Physician, where He touches, He heals. Are you opening yourself to the God of all comfort?

RELATING TRUTH TO LIFE: YOUR COMFORT GRIEF AND GROWTH WORKBOOK

As you limp up to the face of God, your path will be distinctly your own. As you read the following comfort grief and growth exercises, design your own workout routine, selecting the ones that are best for your journey.

In this chapter, I've designed your grief and growth work to help *you* to move from *depression and alienation to comfort and communion*—experiencing the presence of God in the presence of suffering. His presence empowers you to survive scars and plants the seeds of hope that you will yet thrive. I pray that the following exercises will assist you to trace your comfort *journey*—what your path has been like so far and how you can continue to move forward. And I pray that these exercises will help you to map your comfort *journal*—putting words (whether written or thought) to your grief.

YOUR COMFORT JOURNEY

1. In comfort, you tenaciously wrestle with God resulting in painful, yet profitable, comfort through communion. Where would you rate yourself on a scale of 1-10, with 1 being depressed, alienated from God, and giving up on life, and 10 being clinging to God for dear life?

2. In past times of suffering, how did you begin to move from depression and alienation to communion with and comfort in God?

3. Sometimes life beats us down so much and scars us so deeply that we just want to quit. We want to retreat, to give up on God and on ourselves. How are you facing that temptation?

4. In our suffering, God divulges more of Himself. When our heart is grieved, God is the strength of our heart (Psalm 73:21-28). What will it look like for you to acknowledge your grief and to groan to God for His strength?

5. Find a trusted, safe friend and take the step of sharing about your scars with him or her. Ask if he or she would pray for you that the seeds of hope would grow so that you could not only survive, but begin again to thrive.

YOUR COMFORT JOURNAL

1. Jacob's physical wound left him with a permanent limp. Ironically, it left him stronger than ever spiritually. How is that possible? How could that happen in your life?

2. Some wounds won't be totally healed until heaven (Revelation 7). How can you connect to Christ's resurrection power to face life with your wound?

3. What can't be cured can be endured.

   a. Comfort originally meant co-fortitude. How does your connection with Christ fortify you? How does it en-courage you—pour courage into you?

   b. How does communion with Christ help you to say, "Yes, I have a scar, but it is neither fatal nor final"?

4. What is your suffering teaching you about God's power made perfect in your weakness?

5. Christ often comforts us through other Christians. Who is coming alongside to help and comfort you? How could you connect with other Christians so they could help you bear your burdens?

6. Faith perceives that God feels our pain, joins us in our pain, and even shares our pain. In all our distress He is distressed (Isaiah 63:9). Sharing your sorrow with God makes your sorrow endurable. Write a Psalm of Shared Sorrow to God.

7. Which seems harder for you: candor, complaint, cry, or comfort?

   a. Why do you suppose that is?

   b. How could you mature in that area?

YOUR JOURNEY CONTINUES

The journey thus far has brought you to a sign marked "*Surviving*." That's good. Very good. You are a survivor!

It may be hard to believe, but even more is possible. *Thriving* is possible! I know, sometimes it's hard to imagine that you could ever thrive. You think to yourself and of yourself, "*Surviving, maybe. Thriving, I don't see it.*"

Though trapped in a desert outside, through Christ you can be rescued inside—you can drink from His spring of living water. You can be healed through hope—hope that groans for heaven, trusts in God, lives for others, and experiences abundant life.

Hope beckons.

CHAPTER SIX
Waiting: When God Says, "Not Yet"

───◆───

IF THE GRIEF PROCESS WAS A DIRECT JOURNEY, *AND IT IS NOT,* we would be arriving at the halfway point on our path. Sustaining has been the first "half" of our journey—the journey from denial to candor, from anger to complaint, from bargaining to crying out to God, and from depression to comfort.

HEALING: "IT'S POSSIBLE TO HOPE AND SUPERNATURAL TO GROW"

At your "half-way point," you've drawn a line in the sand of retreat so that you can *survive* the onslaught of your loss (sustaining). As you continue your journey, you step over the line so you can *thrive* even while facing your loss (healing). You move forward with a new beginning through renewed faith, hope, grace, and love.

The apostle Paul perfectly models the healing process in the passage we've referenced previously—2 Corinthians 1:8-10. Despairing of life and feeling the sentence of death (sustaining), Paul clings to the Author of life (healing).

> But this happened that we might not rely on ourselves but on God who raises the dead. He has delivered us from such a deadly peril, and he will deliver us. On him we have set our hope that he will continue to deliver us (2 Corinthians 1:9-10).

I'd like to ask you to stop reading. Reflect on Paul's grief *and* on his hope.

Reflect on your grief.

Pray for your healing. Ask for hope. Ask God for the faith to believe that a new beginning is possible—it's possible to hope, to thrive.

Grieving can produce growth. Spiritual emergencies can produce spiritual emergence. It's supernatural to grow.

"Acceptance" and "resignation" are too earthly-minded to be of any earthly or heavenly good!

Sustaining says, *"Life is bad."* Healing says, *"God is good—He's good all the time."* In sustaining, we enter the smaller *earthly, temporal* story of hurt. In healing, we enter the larger, *heavenly, eternal* story of hope.

In sustaining, we're in a casket—the tomb of grief and loss. In healing, God rolls the stone away. We *celebrate the resurrection.* We trust in our God who raises the dead.

"Nice," you think. "Just another batch of platitudes: pie-in-the-sky, sweet-by-and-by, too-heavenly-minded-to-be-of-any-earthly-good!"

Not at all. In fact, biblical hope is so heavenly-minded that it is of great practical earthly good.

Think about the fifth and final phase in the *world's* grieving process: *acceptance.* The goal is to face calmly the finality of loss. If it is one's own impending death, then it's a time of quiet resignation. If it is the loss of a loved one, or a relationship, or a job, then it's a time of regrouping. "Life has to go on, somehow. How? What's next?"

In Christ, loss is never final. Christ's resurrection is the first-fruit of every resurrection. "Acceptance" and "resignation" are too earthly-minded to be of any earthly or heavenly good! Acceptance can't halt retreat because it has no hope for advancement, no foundation for growth.

I refuse to accept the hopeless remedy of acceptance. I also refuse to accept simplistic platitudes. I choose to embrace Christ's healing hope. I choose to embrace the biblical truth that "it's possible to hope and supernatural to grow."

Healing celebrates the resurrection by exploring waiting, wailing, weaving, and worshiping. These four biblical "stages" contrast with and expand upon the one stage in the world's process of acceptance.

HEALING IN SUFFERING: STAGES OF HOPE
"IT'S POSSIBLE TO HOPE AND SUPERNATURAL TO GROW"

Stage	Typical Acceptance Response	Biblical Growth Response
Stage Five	Regrouping	Waiting: Trusting with Faith
Stage Six	Deadening	Wailing: Groaning with Hope
Stage Seven	Despairing/Doubting	Weaving: Perceiving with Grace
Stage Eight	Digging Cisterns	Worshiping: Engaging with Love

In Christ it is possible to trust God with faith, groan to God with hope, perceive suffering with grace, and engage God and others with love, even during suffering. Let's learn how.

WAITING: TRUSTING WITH FAITH RATHER THAN REGROUPING WITH SELF-SUFFICIENCY

You're in a casket. Finally, you've come face-to-face with death and with utter human hopelessness. Do you want to stay there? No! Frantic to escape? Yes! You cry out to God for help. What does He say?

"*Wait.*"

Now you're at a faith-point. "I trust Him; I trust Him not. I'll wait; I'll not wait."

Which will it be? Will you wait or regroup? Will you wait on God or will you self-sufficiently depend upon yourself?

REGROUPING: TAKING MATTERS INTO MY OWN HANDS

John 4 illustrates the contrast between waiting and regrouping. The woman at the well was in a husband-casket. One husband left the scene, "Encore! Encore!" she'd shout, bringing the curtain down on another failed marriage. Frantically she searched time after time for a man she could have—a man she could desperately clutch, who would meet her desperate needs by desperately desiring her above all else.

We don't know what came next for her after she surrendered her thirsts to Christ. Certainly, if she were to live out her new Christ-life, she would have to change her habitual pattern of regrouping through having a man.

Suppose she took her longing to God in prayer. Presuppose God told her to stop living with this man who was not her husband. Don't you think that on a human plane she would experience excruciating emptiness, starving hunger?

So she prays to God, "Father, I know that all I need is You and what You choose to provide. I'm cleaning up my life. Would You please send me a godly man?"

God says, "Wait. Delay your gratification. Don't get involved with a man."

Everything inside her—her flesh-habituated past way of surviving, her cistern-digging style of relating—craves satisfaction *now*. If she regroups, she grasps yet another husband on the rebound. She takes matters into her own hands.

WAITING: REFUSING TO DEMAND HEAVEN NOW

So what would "hope" look like in her immediate context? Hoping in God, she would choose delayed gratification over immediate gratification. She would accept her singleness, clinging to God and trusting His timing.

Hope waits. Hope is the refusal to demand heaven now.

If hope leads to waiting, what then is waiting? *Waiting is trusting God's future provision without working to provide for oneself.* Waiting is refusing to take over while refusing to give up. Waiting refuses self-rescue.

───◆───

WAITING: TRUSTING WITH FAITH

Trusting God's future provision
without working to provide for oneself.
Refusing to take over while refusing to give up.

───◆───

Tony Campolo preaches a message where he repeatedly says, "It's Friday, but Sunday's comin'." He's focusing his audience on Friday-truth: the crucifixion of Christ, and on Sunday-truth: the coming resurrection of Christ.

I would change the metaphor a bit because we aren't living on Friday; we're living on Saturday. Symbolically, life lived on fallen planet Earth is Saturday living—the day between the crucifixion and the resurrection. The day of waiting. The day that tests our trust.

You'll never see waiting as one of the stages in any research study because it is not natural in a fallen world. It is supernatural.

TIM AND TERRI'S WAITING JOURNEY: ON THE REBOUND

I once worked with a missionary couple (we'll call them Tim and Terri) whose mission agency refused to allow them to return to the field. In essence, they were fired without cause. Frankly, the situation appeared to be nothing more than a power struggle.

We were working through the candor, complaint, cry, and comfort process. When we began to explore the waiting stage, Tim battled. Everything in him wanted, almost desperately needed, to regroup.

He was ready to join a ministry, any ministry, on the rebound. He was ready to take a job, any job. However, I counseled him to wait before making any long-term commitments to a new ministry position because I sensed he was motivated by a desire for self-rescue, for regrouping, not by a desire to wait on God.

BIBLICAL WAITING SAMPLERS: CLINGING TO GOD'S ROPE OF HOPE

Was my counsel godly or ungodly? Wise or foolish? Too heavenly-minded to be of any earthly good? Can we find biblical support for the principle of waiting rather than regrouping?

Waiting is rooted in the Old Testament. The Prophets promised Israel that a better day was coming, *later*. The New Testament writers develop the waiting theme when they urge us toward patience, perseverance, longsuffering, and remaining under (Romans 5; James 1; 1 Peter 1-2; and Hebrews 11).

***

*In waiting, we cling to God's rope of hope,
even when we can't see it.*

***

In waiting, we cling to God's rope of hope, even when we can't see it. In biblical waiting, we neither numb our longings nor illegitimately fulfill them.

WAITING'S EVIL TWIN: IMMEDIATE GRATIFICATION

The opposite of waiting is meeting my "needs" *now*, taking matters into my own hands now, and acting as if I'm my only hope. Esau embodies regrouping through immediate gratification (Hebrews 12:16). For a single meal, a bowl of soup, he sold his birthright. He refused to look ahead, to wait, to delay gratification.

What is your bowl of soup? Mine? What am I convinced that I must have *now* that I believe is more pleasing to my deepest appetite than God and what He chooses to provide and what He promises?

In the context of grief, regrouping through self-gratification says, "I have to feel better *now*! Things *must* be the same as they once were!" We want to be our own genie in a bottle—granting ourselves two wishes: changed feelings and changed circumstances.

REMEMBERING THE FUTURE: NO TURKISH DELIGHT

Moses exemplifies delayed gratification and waiting.

By faith Moses, when he had grown up, refused to be known as the son of Pharaoh's daughter. He *chose to be mistreated* along with the people of *God rather than to enjoy the pleasures of sin for a short time.* He regarded disgrace for the sake of Christ as of greater value than the treasures of Egypt, *because he was looking ahead to his reward* (Hebrews 11:24-26, emphasis added).

No quick fix for Moses. No "Turkish Delight" from the White Witch of Narnia. No pleasures of sin for a season. Why? How could he wait? He chose eternal pleasure over temporal happiness. *He remembered the future.*

Faith looks *back* to the past recalling God's mighty works saying, "He did it that time; He can do it now." Hope looks *ahead* remembering God's coming reward saying, "I consider that our present sufferings are not worth comparing with the glory that will be revealed in us. The creation *waits* in eager expectation for the sons of God to be revealed" (Romans 8:18-19, emphasis added).

In the context of grief, waiting through delayed gratification says, "I want to feel better. I wish things were the way they once were. But I trust God's good heart. I know one day He will wipe away all tears. I know today He has good plans for my life ahead." Instead of viewing God as our genie in a bottle or as a butler at our beck and call, we yield to, trust in, and wait upon God as our Father of holy love.

ON THE ROAD TO HOPE

On the road to hope we encounter many choice points, many forks in the road. Your current choice is life altering: will you trust God or trust yourself? Will you demand heaven now or wait for heavenly hope?

Everything within us feels as if taking matters into our own hands, meeting our own needs, quenching our own thirsts, and numbing our own pain is the answer. The world, the flesh, and the devil happily cheer us on.

But it's all a mirage. Regrouping is nothing more than retreating. It's backtracking. It's a sophisticated, self-sufficient form of denial. And who wants to head back to the beginning of the journey?

Instead of turning back, *look back with eyes of faith* to recall how God has rescued you in the past. Instead of trusting in yourself, trust in God and *look ahead with eyes of hope* to remember the future God beckons you toward.

RELATING TRUTH TO LIFE: YOUR WAITING GRIEF AND GROWTH WORKBOOK

Just as your "sustaining" journey was personal, unique, and distinctively your own, so your "healing" journey will be also. As you read the following waiting growth exercises, create your own personal workout routine, selecting the ones that are best for your journey.

In this chapter, I've designed your growth work to help *you* move from *regrouping and self-sufficiency to waiting and God-sufficiency*—trusting God's future provision without working to provide for yourself. Waiting on God empowers you to refuse to take over while refusing to give up.

I pray that the following exercises will assist you to trace your waiting *journey*—what your path has been like so far and how you can continue to move forward. And I pray that these exercises will help you to develop your waiting *journal*—putting words (whether written or thought) to your growth—grieving with hope.

YOUR WAITING JOURNEY

1. In waiting, you refuse to take over while refusing to give up. Where would you rate yourself on a scale of 1-10, with 1 being demanding immediate, self-sufficient gratification—changed feelings and circumstances, and with 10 being waiting on God by delaying gratification through faith?

2. When God wanted Esau to wait, Esau took matters into his own hands and messed everything up. Are you facing any similar temptations to handle your hurt on your own? To fix things in your own strength?

3. In past times of suffering, how did you begin to move from regrouping and self-sufficiency to waiting, faith, and God-sufficiency?

4. Think back to a time when God brought hope, joy, newness, and "resurrection" into your life after a casket experience.

    a. What did God use to bring about your spiritual victory?

    b. How did you begin to see God differently? How did you begin to experience more of His goodness? How were you able to love Him more deeply?

    c. As you found His strength in your weakness, what was God able to accomplish through you? How was He able to use you as a hero/heroine in His grand adventure narrative?

5. You're at a faith-point. "I trust Him; I trust Him not. I'll wait; I'll not wait." Which will it be? Will you wait or regroup? Will you wait on God or will you depend upon yourself?

6. Find a trusted, safe friend and take the step of sharing your hopes and dreams with him or her. Share also your temptation to take matters into your own hands, along with your desire to wait on God and His perfect timing.

YOUR WAITING JOURNAL

1. God's timing and ours are often light years apart. What are you experiencing as you wait on God?

2. Hope waits. What are you waiting on God for? How are you trusting God's future provision without taking matters into your own hands?

3. What would it look like for you to rest in God right now? For you to surrender to God? To trust instead of work, to wait instead of demand?

4. Someone once defined biblical perseverance as "remaining under without giving in." How are you remaining under your suffering without giving in to self-rescue? Where are you finding the strength to do that?

5. Waiting is refusing to take over while refusing to give up. Where are you finding the strength to "keep on keeping on"? How are you resisting the temptation to "curse God and die"?

6. Explore passages like Romans 5; James 1; 1 Peter 1, and Hebrews 11 that teach how to wait on God in the midst of suffering. Paraphrase their message for your life today.

7. How could you apply Moses' delayed gratification, waiting, faith, and trust (Hebrews 11:24-26) to your situation?

8. Paul considered that his present sufferings were not worth comparing with the glory that will be revealed in us (Romans 8:18-19). What future glory are you focusing on?

9. Read Revelation 7. How do these wonderful pictures of heaven give you hope today?

YOUR JOURNEY CONTINUES

When we wait, and wait, and wait . . . and we still find no answers, no fulfillment this side of heaven, what results? How are we to respond? What do "growth" and "healing" look like while we wait?

Must we return to denial and numbing? Are we to do nothing at all? What does God expect? What does He want of us? How are we supposed to handle the ache of our soul?

All honest, good, fair questions. All to be addressed as we explore *Wailing: Pregnant with Hope.*

CHAPTER SEVEN

Wailing: Pregnant with Hope

—————

WHEN WE CRY OUT TO GOD, HE PROMISES HIS COMFORT. However, He does not promise "quick answers." He is a "time God." He does not come before time. He does not come after time. He comes at just the right time. And . . . He comes in His way for His glory and our good.

So, when His timing and our timing are light years apart, we wait. We resist the temptation to regroup and to fix things on our own.

WAILING: GROANING WITH HOPE RATHER THAN DEADENING

But let's be honest. Waiting brings more pain. We're then tempted to deaden the pain as we wait for God's healing hope. That's why in stage six of the grieving and growth process we must move from deadening our pain to *wailing: groaning with hope*.

The barren Shunammite woman of 2 Kings 4 helps us to picture the deadening process. After years of barrenness, she bears a son who fulfills a lifetime of hopes and dreams.

Tragically, he dies. Life has sent her two caskets: the first one—her inability to conceive; the second one—the death of the child she finally bore.

Rather than facing her loss, she keeps repeating, "It's all right." Her heart is sick, her soul is vexed, yet she keeps insisting, "It's all right. I'm all right."

Have you "been there, done that"? I have. Faking it. Pretending. But we can't play make-believe forever.

Eventually it all spills out like it did for the Shunammite woman. She finally screams at Elisha, "Did I not say to you, 'Don't deceive me! Don't get my *hopes* up'?" Deadening refuses to hope ever again, to dream ever again.

Hope deferred makes the heart sick (Proverbs 13:12). Hope hoped for, received, then lost again, makes the heart deathly ill. Fragile. Needy.

WAILING: GROANING WITH HOPE

Longing fervently for heaven and *living passionately for God and others while on earth.*

We hate being there, so we block it out. We deaden ourselves by refusing to hope, long, wail, or groan because groaning exposes us as the needy people we are.

The problem is that God made us longing, thirsting, hungering, desiring beings. So we follow a trillion different strategies for deadening our desires and shutting out the wail of our soul. We live as if this world is all there is. We refuse to hope for something more. We make it our goal to satisfy the flesh in order to quench the ache in our soul—the ache of our loss.

WAILING: STAYING ALIVE TO LIFE WHEN IT CRUSHES YOU TO DEATH

So what are we supposed to do? We wail. It is through *wailing* that we stay alive to life even when it tries to crush us to death. By wailing, I don't mean weeping as in the candor, complaint, or cry of sustaining, though weeping often accompanies wailing.

"I ache for Paradise.
But I'm pulling weeds until the day I die!"

What then is wailing? Wailing is *longing fervently for heaven* **and** *living passionately for God and others while still on earth.*
Paul personifies wailing in Philippians 1:23-25.

> I am torn between the two: I *desire to depart and be with Christ,* which is better by far; but it is more necessary for you that I remain in the body. Convinced of this, I know that I will remain, and *I will continue with all of you for your progress* and joy in the faith (emphasis added).

Paul neither deadens his longing for heaven nor minimizes his calling on earth.

Wailing is longing, hungering, thirsting, and wanting what is legitimate, what is promised, but what we do not have. It is grieving the "not yet" without giving up on the "now."

How is wailing different from candor and complaint?

In candor, I admit that "I hate what has happened to me."

In complaint, I say, "God, I'm confused and devastated by what has happened to me."

In wailing, I groan, "I wanna' go home. This world is so messed up. I ache for Paradise. But I'm pulling weeds until the day I die!"

TIM AND TERRI'S WAILING JOURNEY: "I'M NOT GONNA' STOP DREAMING!"

In the situation with the missionary couple, Terri knew how to groan. She told me once, "Bob, everything in me wants to tell Tim never, ever to go into the ministry again. He's so wounded, and I'm so scared for him. Everything in me wants to say, 'I'll never be a ministry spouse again.'"

Then she leaned forward with a glimmer in her eyes as she said,

I watched the *Les Miserables* DVD you loaned me. Fantine sang, "There are some storms you cannot weather," and "Life has killed the dream I dreamed." By God's grace, that's not going to happen to me. I'm not going to quit feeling. I'm not going to quit living. I'm not going to quit connecting. I've experienced a taste of the fellowship of Christ's suffering and I'll never be the same. I'm more alive today than I have ever been in my life. God's given me a vision of ministering to other women, to ministry wives.

Then she leaned back, engulfed in a restful, confident smile, almost a smirk. It's been five years now. God has been fulfilling Terri's ministry dream.

God calls us to keep longing for Paradise while still pulling weeds even while we live east of Eden. God calls us to keep dreaming even after life tries to kill our dreams.

Are you pulling weeds? Are you dreaming? Are you wailing—ready to go home, but committed to zealous living until the day you die?

BIBLICAL WAILING SAMPLERS:
HOW TO BE A *NIKE* CHRISTIAN

Is wailing a biblical response to our suffering? Where does God tell us to *long fervently for heaven **and** live passionately for God and others while still on earth?* What Scriptures teach us how to groan with hope?

DESPERATE DESIRE

Consider Romans 8:18-25 and its support for wailing as part of God's plan for responding to suffering.

I consider that our *present sufferings* are not worth comparing with the glory that will be revealed in us. The creation waits in eager expectation for the sons of God to be revealed. For the creation was subjected to *frustration*, not by its own choice, but by the will of the one who subjected it, *in hope* that the creation itself will be liberated from its bondage to decay, and brought into the glorious freedom of the children of God. We know that the whole creation has been *groaning* as in the pains of *childbirth* right up to the present time. Not only so, but we ourselves, who have the first fruits of the Spirit, *groan inwardly as we wait eagerly* for our adoption as sons, the redemption of our bodies. For in this hope we were saved. But hope that is seen is no hope at all. Who hopes for what he already has? But if we hope for what we do not yet have, we wait for it patiently (emphasis added).

Designed for Paradise, we live in a desert. No wonder we are thirsty. No wonder we groan for heaven. We might picture the big picture like this:

- Paradise: "Now!" Full
- Desert: "No!" Empty
- Thirst: "Not Yet!" Groaning

Everything was very good and completely satisfying in Paradise. God gifted Adam and Eve with all they needed and so much more. They were full.

Then, because they refused to rest in God's fullness, they were barricaded from the Garden, sent roaming east of Eden into the desert. Instead of the happy cry of "Now! All my needs are met now!" they now cry, "No! We are empty. Thirsty. Hungry."

Created for Paradise and living in a desert, they and their offspring become thirsty. Our new cry is "Not yet!" We say, "I want what I want and I want it now." God says, "I promise you that I will quench all your legitimate thirsts, *but not yet.*"

OUT OF THE NEST

So we wail and we groan.

What types of groans? In Romans 8:18-25, Paul joins suffering, frustration, eager waiting, and pregnant groaning.

"Frustration" suggests the ache that we feel because of the emptiness and void we experience, living in a fallen world. It's the same Greek word used to translate Solomon's word "vanity"—meaningless, soap bubbles, unsatisfying, pointless, absurd—all of this describes life south of heaven.

"Eager waiting" pictures ferocious, desperate desire. When we wail, we declare how deeply out of the nest we are, how far from home we've wandered, and how much we long for heaven.

When we wail, we declare how deeply out of the nest we are . . . and how much we long for heaven.

Paul illustrates our desperate desire using the imagery of pregnancy. He describes a woman groaning in labor that lasts not hours, not nine months, but a lifetime. Imagine a pregnant woman in labor for 70 years! That's groaning. Groaning not only the pain of seemingly unending labor, but *groaning the pain of not having the joy of the baby*.

That's our current condition. For our allotted years on this blue planet, we're *pregnant with hope*, groaning for Paradise, for Eden, for walking with God in the cool of the day, for being naked and unashamed, for shalom.

When we groan and wail, we admit to ourselves and express to God the pain of our unmet desires, the depth of our fervent longing for heaven's joy, and our total commitment to remain pregnant with hope—labor for a lifetime.

THRIVING

And what's the result? Weak, mournful surviving? No way! The result is thriving.

In Romans 8:28-39, Paul insists that even in the midst of trouble, hardship, persecution, and suffering, nothing can separate us from the love of God in Christ Jesus. He teaches that in all our suffering we are more than conquerors through Him who loved us so.

"More than conquerors" comes from the Greek word *nikao* from which we gain our word "Nike"—victors, winners, Olympic champions. Wailing empowers us to long ardently for heaven and to live victoriously on earth. Wailing moves us from victims to victors in Christ.

ON THE ROAD TO HOPE

You've just encountered another choice point on the road to hope. At this fork in the road, you can turn one direction and choose the journey of deadening. Taking that route, your pain never goes away; it's just buried beneath any number of self-protective diversions.

Or, you can choose the route of wailing and groaning with hope. You'll feel the pain—the deep pain of being out of the nest, of living east of Eden, of longing fervently for heaven but living in our fallen world. However, you'll experience the profound joy that accompanies living passionately for God and others. God's Spirit will empower your spirit so you can be more than a conqueror—now!

RELATING TRUTH TO LIFE: YOUR WAILING GRIEF AND GROWTH WORKBOOK

As you read the following wailing grief and growth exercises, create your own personal workout routine, selecting the journey assignments and the journal questions that are best for you. In this chapter, I've designed your growth work to help *you* to move from *deadening to wailing and groaning with hope*—longing fervently for heaven *and* living passionately for God and others while on earth.

I pray that the following exercises will assist you to trace your wailing *journey*—what your path has been like so far and how you can continue to move forward. And I pray that these exercises will help you develop your wailing *journal*—putting words (whether written or thought) to your growth—grieving with hope.

YOUR WAILING JOURNEY

1. In wailing, you refuse to deaden the pain of your loss and you choose to wail and groan with hope. Where would you rate yourself on a scale of 1-10, with 1 being deadening pain with self-protective numbing strategies and 10 being longing fervently for heaven and living passionately for God and others on earth?

2. In past times of suffering, how did you begin to move from deadening to wailing?

3. When are you most tempted to deaden the pain of life? How do you defeat this temptation so you're able to groan to God?

4. The temptation when life beats us down is to refuse to face life anymore. We barely survive, rather than victoriously thrive. How can you victoriously thrive?

5. Find a trusted, safe friend and take the step of sharing your longing for heaven with him or her. Let your friend hear how you are wailing and groaning with hope.

YOUR WAILING JOURNAL

1. God made you a longing, thirsting, hungering, desiring being. What God-designed thirst is your loss stirring up in your soul?

2. Groaning exposes us for the needy people we are. How hard is it for you to admit your neediness—to yourself, to others, and to God?

3. If you were to write a thirst psalm like Psalm 42, how would you word it?

4. As Paul faced suffering, he groaned for heaven (Romans 8:17-25). What are you groaning for?

5. In Romans 8:17-18, Paul did some spiritual mathematics and reasoned that his current sufferings were not worth comparing with his future glory. As you calculate your earthly suffering and your eternal glory, what conclusions do you make?

6. Reread and meditate upon Philippians 1:23-25. Paul says that he longs for heaven, but that he's passionate about staying on earth in order to glorify God and benefit others. What would it look like in your grieving to apply this passage to your life?

7. Satan wants to use your suffering to suck the life out of you. How can you connect to Christ's resurrection power to find new life, new zeal for God? How can you not only survive, but thrive?

8. God calls you to keep longing for Paradise while still pulling weeds, even while you live east of Eden. What weeds is God calling you to pull?

YOUR JOURNEY CONTINUES

Surely we can't stay forever in the wailing stage. How do we uncover God's perspective on life? How do we gain the spiritual eyes, the faith eyes, to see life with 20/20 spiritual vision again?

We need spiritual laser surgery. It is in the grieving and growing stage of *Weaving* that the Divine Soul Physician operates on the eyes of our hearts. We visit His office next.

CHAPTER EIGHT
Weaving: Spiritual Mathematics

TO UNDERSTAND OUR JOURNEY, LET'S TRACK THE WORLD'S typical grief and acceptance process thus far. Suffering crashes upon us. In shock, we *deny* its reality. At some point, our emotions can no longer suppress the truth and we explode with *anger*. Anger doesn't get us what we want, so we switch tactics and try *bargaining*—behaving, being good, and doing good works. However, in spite of everything we try, we can't manage our loss. *Depression* sets in, alienation strikes.

At some point, the depression lifts a tad. We figure that we have to get on with life somehow. So we *regroup*. We re-enter the game, not with a new heart, but with no other choice. The game's still rough, it still hurts, so we do what we can to *deaden* and suppress the pain—maybe work-a-holism, maybe ministry-a-holism, anything and everything.

WEAVING: PERCEIVING WITH GRACE RATHER THAN DESPAIRING/DOUBTING

But like the Shunammite woman, we're assaulted by life again, only worse. None of our strategies work. Now what? What do we think? What do we do? What do we feel?

Since we pursue what we perceive to be pleasing, it all depends upon our perspective. Do we perceive with grace eyes or with despairing eyes?

DESPAIR: THE NEGATIVE OF HOPE

If we attempt to handle our loss without Christ, we *despair*. We *doubt*. We give up any hope of ever making life work, of ever figuring out the mystery of life, or of ever completing the puzzle. We trudge on in doubt, despair, and darkness. *Despair is the negative of hope.*

That's the world's typical response. It is *not* God's healing path. In God's growth voyage we move from regrouping to waiting (stage five), from deadening to wailing (stage six), and from despairing to weaving (stage seven)—perceiving with grace.

WEAVING: PERCEIVING WITH GRACE

Entrusting myself to God's larger purposes, good plans, and eternal perspective.

WEAVING: SEE IN THIS SOME HIGHER PLAN

Our eyes darkened by despair, we need grace-eyes. We need to weave in another way of looking at life.

Biblical weaving is *entrusting myself to God's larger purposes, good plans, and eternal perspective.* I see life with spiritual eyes instead of eyeballs only. I look at suffering, not with rose-colored glasses, but with faith eyes, with Cross-eyes, with 20/20 spiritual vision.

When Terri told me about the growth in her life, I asked her what made the difference, what helped her to turn the corner. She responded, "Two things. No, two people. The bishop and Joseph."

While Terri was watching *Les Miserables*, she was struck by the scene where Jean val Jean, a paroled prisoner, takes advantage of the grace-filled Bishop of Digne. After stealing from him, Jean val Jean is captured by the French police. They return him to the bishop, fully expecting him to implicate val Jean, which would lead to a return to prison without hope for parole. To the shock of everyone involved, the bishop says, "But my brother, you forgot these," and hands him two silver candlesticks.

As Terri put it. "I was floored when the Bishop sang, 'By the witness and the martyrs, by the passion and the blood, I have bought your soul for God. Now become an honest man. See in this some higher plan.' Val Jean, amazed by grace, changed by grace, concludes the scene by singing, 'Another story must begin!'"

Terri, recounting this to me, continued. "Now in everything that happens to me, I'm looking for God's higher plan. I'm setting my thoughts on things above—always wondering what God might be up to in this. For me, another story must begin—God's story that doesn't obliterate my painful story, but that gives it meaning."

BIBLICAL WEAVING SAMPLERS: LIFE IS BAD, BUT GOD IS GOOD

How does Terri's approach mirror God's process of grieving with hope? We find weaving woven into the fabric of Scripture from Genesis to Revelation (Genesis 50, John 14, Romans 8, Ephesians 3, Colossians 3, Hebrews 11, and Revelation 19-22).

JOSEPH'S STORY

Recall that Terri had referred to the bishop *and* to Joseph. Hear Joseph's words to his fearful family in Genesis 50:19-20: "Don't be afraid. Am I in the place of God? You intended to harm me, but God intended it for good to accomplish what is now being done, the saving of many lives."

Joseph uses "intended" both for his brothers' plans and God's purposes. The Hebrew word has a very tangible sense of to weave, to plait, to interpenetrate as in the weaving together of fabric to fashion a robe, perhaps even Joseph's coat of many colors.

The Old Testament also used the word in a negative, metaphorical sense to suggest a malicious plot, the devising of a cruel scheme. Other times the Jews used "intended" to picture symbolically the creation of some new and beautiful purpose or result through the weaving together of seemingly haphazard, miscellaneous, or malicious events.

"Life is bad," Joseph admits. "You plotted against me for *evil*. You *intended* to spoil or ruin something wonderful."

"God is good," Joseph insists. "God wove good out of evil," choosing a word for "good" that is the superlative of pleasant, beautiful. That is, God *intended* to create amazing beauty from seemingly worthless ashes for those who grieve (Isaiah 61:3).

GRACE NARRATIVES: WEAVING TRUTH INTO LIFE

Joseph discovers healing through God's grace narrative. Further, he offers his brothers tastes of grace.

> And now, do not be distressed and do not be angry with yourselves for selling me here, because it was to save lives that God sent me ahead of you. For two years now there has been famine in the land, and for the next five years there will not be plowing and reaping. But God sent me ahead of you to preserve for you a remnant on earth and to save your lives by a great deliverance. So then, it was not you who sent me here, but God. He made me father to Pharaoh, lord of his entire household and ruler of all Egypt (Genesis 45:5-8).

Amazing! I hope you caught the words. "To save lives," "to preserve," "by a great deliverance." That's a grace narrative, a salvation narrative. Had God not preserved a remnant of Abraham's descendants, Jesus would never have been born. Joseph uses his spiritual eyes to see God's great grace purposes in saving not only Israel and Egypt, but also the entire world.

I hope you also caught Joseph's repetition. "God sent me." "God sent me ahead of you." "It was not you who sent me here, but God." Joseph sees the smaller story of human scheming for ruin. However, he also perceives that God trumps that smaller scheme with His larger purpose by weaving beauty out of ugly.

Life hurts. Wounds penetrate. Without grace narratives, hopelessness and bitterness flourish. With a grace narrative, hope and forgiveness flow and perspective grows.

Instead of our perspective shrinking, suffering is the exact time when we must listen most closely, when we must lean over to hear the whisper of God. True, God shouts to us in our pain, but His answers, as with Elijah, often come to us in whispered still small voices amid the thunders of the world.

Instead of our perspective shrinking, suffering is the exact time when we must listen most closely, when we must lean over to hear the whisper of God.

In weaving, God heals our wounds as we envision a future even while all seems lost in the present. Through hope we remember the future; we move from Good Friday to Easter Sunday while living on Saturday. Grace narratives point the way to God's larger story, assuring us that our Savior is worth our wait.

GRACE MATH: DIVINE CALCULATIONS

Healing wounds requires grace narratives *and* grace math. Grace math teaches us that *present suffering plus God's character equals future glory*. The equation we use is the divine perspective.

From a Divine faith perspective on life, we erect a platform to respond to suffering. How we view life makes all the difference in how we respond to life's losses. Martin Luther understood this. "The Holy Spirit knows that a thing only has such value and meaning to a man as he assigns it in his thoughts."[1]

We must reshape our interpretation of life by contemplating suffering from a new grace perspective. Through God's Word we nurture alternative ways to view life's losses.

The spiritual consolation offered by Scripture is a new vision, the power of faith to see suffering and death from the viewpoint of our crucified and risen Lord. It renews our sight and turns our common human view of matters upside down. This does not eradicate the pain or the fear of misery; it robs it of its hopelessness.[2]

Our earth-bound, non-faith human story of suffering must yield to God's narrative of life and suffering—to God's grace narrative and grace math. Luther beautifully portrays the God-perspective that prompts healing.

> If only a man could see his God in such a light of love . . . how happy, how calm, how safe he would be! He would then truly have a God from whom he would know with certainty that all his fortunes—whatever they might be—had come to him and were still coming to him under the guidance of God's most gracious will.[3]

As you respond to your loss, are you struggling to believe that God has a good heart? Look to the Cross. The Cross forever settles all questions about God's heart for us. According to Luther, without faith in God's grace through Christ's death, we are tone-deaf to God-reality.

> He who does not believe that he is forgiven by the inexhaustible riches of Christ's righteousness is like a deaf man hearing a story. If we consider it properly and with an attentive heart, this one image—even if there were no other—would suffice to fill us with such comfort that we should not only not grieve over our evils, but should also glory in our tribulations, scarcely feeling them for the joy that we have in Christ.[4]

The Christ of the Cross is the only One who makes sense of life when suffering bombards us.

ON THE ROAD TO HOPE

Weaving is the next choice point you encounter on the road to hope. You can look at your losses with "eyeballs only"—with the world's narrative and the world's math. But in doing so, you'll crop

Christ out of the picture. And whenever you crop out Christ, you crop out hope. Despair and doubt then reign.

Or, approaching this fork in the road, you can crop Christ back into the picture. You can do some spiritual mathematics through grace narratives and grace math. With spiritual eyes you can trust God's good heart. Jeremiah's conviction (and consider all the suffering he endured) can become yours. "'For I know the plans I have for you,' declares the Lord, 'plans to prosper you and not to harm you, plans to give you hope and a future'" (Jeremiah 29:11).

Relating Truth to Life: Your Weaving Grief and Growth Workbook

As you read the following weaving grief and growth exercises, create your own personal workout routine, selecting the *journey* assignments and the *journal* questions that are best for you. In this chapter, I've designed your growth work to help *you* to move from *doubt and despair to weaving and perceiving with grace*—entrusting yourself to God's larger purposes, good plans, and eternal perspective.

I pray that the following exercises will assist you to trace your weaving *journey*—what your path has been like so far and how you can continue to move forward. And I pray that these exercises will help you to develop your weaving *journal*—putting words (whether written or thought) to your growth—grieving with hope.

Your Weaving Journey

1. In weaving, you refuse to give in to despair and you choose to perceive life with grace eyes and grace math. Where would you rate yourself on a scale of 1-10, with 1 being doubting God's good heart and despairing of hope, and 10 being entrusting yourself to God's larger purposes, good plans, and eternal perspective?

2. In past times of suffering, how did you begin to move from doubt and despair to weaving—perceiving with grace?

3. When else have you experienced suffering like this? What did you learn about God in that situation? What would you repeat and what would you change?

4. How could you look at your suffering, not with rose-colored glasses, but with faith eyes, with Cross-eyes, with 20/20 spiritual vision—grace narratives and grace math?

5. Find a trusted, safe friend and take the step of discussing with him or her your two main ways of interpreting your life losses: with eyeballs only or with spiritual eyes.

YOUR WEAVING JOURNAL

1. What passages have you found helpful in gaining a new perspective on your suffering?

2. God is all-powerful, holy, good, loving, and in control of everything. What impact do those characteristics of God have on you as you face your loss?

3. How could you apply Genesis 50:19-20 to your life? "Don't be afraid. Am I in the place of God? You intended to harm me, but God intended it for good to accomplish what is now being done, the saving of many lives."

4. What might God be up to in your suffering? How could He be weaving good out of the evil you are experiencing?

5. Life hurts. Wounds penetrate. Without grace narratives, hopelessness and bitterness flourish. With a grace narrative, how could hope flow and your grace perspective grow?

6. God promises that all things work together for good for His children (Romans 8:28). What good purposes has God already provided to you or in you through these events?

7. God's story doesn't obliterate your painful story, but it gives it meaning. What meaning could you find as you weave God's story into yours?

THE JOURNEY CONTINUES

It's been a long road getting from there to here—from denial to perceiving with grace. But even the greatness of a grace narrative is not your final destination. Your final destination is not a place, but a person, the Person—God.

The God of all comfort doesn't just offer you comfort; He offers *Himself*. Find God in your loss. *Worship*—engage God and others with love—even in your grief.

CHAPTER NINE
Worshiping: Finding God

———

TRAVELING FROM GRIEF TO GROWTH IS A LONG, WINDING ROAD.
But we're almost home. As we've progressed through the stages of
healing, God has been transforming us from regrouping to waiting,
from deadening to wailing, from despair to weaving, and now from
digging cisterns to worshiping. To understand cistern-digging, trace
with me the world's grieving path one final time.

WORSHIPING: ENGAGING WITH LOVE
RATHER THAN DIGGING CISTERNS

Finding ourselves in a casket of loss and suffering, we're tempted to
claw our way out through immediate gratification. Our bowl of soup
may be power, prestige, pleasure, people-pleasing, or any multitude
of pathways. Since soup never satisfies the soul, only the stomach,
our ache remains and we're still left with the question and the quest,
"What do we do with our hurt?"

If we face our agony, we're forced to admit our insufficiency. That simply will not do. So we deaden it. We block out and suppress the reality of our hungry heart. Keep busy. Fantasize. Climb the corporate ladder. These tricks of the world's trade work no better than immediate gratification. Somewhere, deep down inside, despair brews. "Is this all there is?"

DIGGING CISTERNS: PURSUING FALSE LOVERS

Now what? If we follow the beaten path, despair guides us to false lovers. Idols of the heart. Digging cisterns, broken cisterns that can hold no water. Something or someone who will rescue us from agony's clutches—or so we imagine.

God describes digging cisterns in Jeremiah 2:13: "My people have committed two sins: they have forsaken me, the spring of living water, and have dug cisterns, broken cisterns that cannot hold water."

In the Ancient Near East, you had two choices for life-giving water. You could settle near a clear, pure, bubbling spring of fresh underground water, or you could dig a cistern that captured run-off water and held it in a stagnant well that often cracked, leaking in more filth and leaking out water.

Spiritual cistern digging involves rejecting God as our Spring of Living Water because we see Him as unsatisfying, unholy, and unloving (Jeremiah 2:5, 19, 31). Once we reject the only Being in the universe who could ever satisfy the last aching abyss of our souls, we choose to turn to substitutes—worthless, putrid, empty, futile substitutes—cisterns.

Now what? Is that all there is?

Not at all. God offers us so much more, infinitely more—because He offers Himself.

WORSHIPING: GLIMPSING THE FACE OF GOD

Now we're ready to map God's grieving and growth process one final time. Your path toward God during suffering also begins with the casket of loss. Finding yourself in that casket, you've been waiting on God, wailing out to God, and weaving together His good plans from His good heart.

Rather than turning to false lovers who tame your soul, you now turn to your untamed God who captures your soul. You worship God. In the midst of life's losses, *yes, you can* choose worship—engaging God with love, which leads to ministry—engaging others with God's love.

"Worship" is such a common word. But what is worship really? Specifically, in the midst of grief, what does worship look like?

Let's start with some subtle contrasts.

In crying, you cry out for God's *help*. In worship, you cry out for *God*.

In comfort, you receive God's *strength*. In worship, you receive *God*.

In wailing, you long for *heaven* because you're tired of earth. In worship, you long for *God* because you miss Him.

In weaving, you glimpse God's *perspective*. In worship, you glimpse the *face of God*.

WORSHIPING: ENGAGING WITH LOVE

Wanting God more than wanting relief.
Finding God even when you don't find answers.

So what is worship in the context of suffering? Worship is *wanting God more than wanting relief*. Worship is *finding God even when you don't find answers*. Worship is *walking with God in the dark and having Him as the light of your soul*.

TIM AND TERRI'S JOURNEY: "NOT EVERYTHING'S PERFECT!"

I received an e-mail from Terri. She began with words I'm sure she typed with a smile. "Guess what? Not everything's perfect in our new ministry." I smiled knowingly as I read her first line.

She continued, "But God is perfect. He is perfectly beautiful. Perfectly holy. Perfectly in control. Perfectly good." Terri is glimpsing the face of God. She's worshiping.

Terri understands the truth that every problem is an opportunity to know God better and our primary battle is to know God well. Thus, if we want our suffering to lead to worship, we have to ask ourselves a primary soul care question, *"How are these problems influencing my relationship to God?"* Problems can either shove us far from God or drag us, kicking and screaming, closer to Him.

BIBLICAL WORSHIPING SAMPLERS: WHOM HAVE I IN HEAVEN BUT YOU?

The Bible consistently invites us to worship God in the midst of suffering. Worship as the end result of suffering has always been the testimony of God's people.

Asaph, reflecting on his suffering, concludes, "Whom have I in heaven but you? And earth has nothing I desire besides you" (Psalm 73:25).

David concurs, as his suffering creates a God-thirst. "As the deer pants for streams of water, so my soul pants for you, O God. My soul thirsts for God, for the living God. When can I go and meet with God?" (Psalm 42:1-2).

Peter acknowledges the ever-present reality of suffering. ". . . you may have had to suffer grief in all kinds of trials" (1 Peter 1:6). He continues by explaining the purpose of problems, teaching that they come so our faith in God may be refined. Peter then shares suffering's significance: "Though you have not seen him, you love him; and even though you do not see him now, you believe in him and are filled with an inexpressible and glorious joy" (1 Peter 1:8).

Peter's message reminds us of Paul as he looks back upon a lifetime of suffering and says:

> I consider everything a loss compared to the surpassing greatness of knowing Christ Jesus my Lord, for whose sake I have lost all things. I consider them rubbish that I may gain Christ. ...I want to know Christ and the power of his resurrection and the fellowship of sharing in his sufferings, becoming like him in his death (Philippians 3:8, 10).

What these biblical writers present, the hymn writer Katharina von Schlegel poetically states:

Be still, my soul! the Lord is on thy side;
Bear patiently the cross of grief or pain;
Leave to thy God to order and provide;
In every change He faithful will remain.
Be still, my soul! the best thy heavenly Friend,
Thro' thorny ways leads to a joyful end.

Suffering's ultimate goal is worship: exalting and enjoying God as our Spring of Living Water—our only satisfaction and our greatest joy.

Finding God and experiencing His love, we're nourished and empowered *so that* we can love others. This was Peter's exact point near the end of his sermon on suffering. The refining fires of suffering purify "so that you have sincere love for your brothers, love one another deeply, from the heart" (1 Peter 1:22).

ON THE ROAD TO HOPE

Think about the difference between the "last best hope" the world offers us in suffering and the "sure hope" God's Word and way promises us. The world can hope for changed circumstances and changed feelings. Maybe they come, maybe they don't. Either way, our lot in life is to "accept" our lot in life. We move on as best we can, making the most we can out of what's left of our life after our loss.

For those who place their sure hope in Christ and His resurrection power, the casket of loss is never final. That's why Peter concludes his sermon on suffering with the words, "For you have been born again, not of perishable seed, but of imperishable, through the living and enduring word of God" (1 Peter 1:23). Our "lot in life" is not "acceptance." It is newness! It is new life and new power—the power to love God and others—worship and ministry.

Satan schemes to use suffering to suck the life out of your soul. God intends to employ creative suffering to enliven your soul. The mini and major caskets of your life losses do not have to lead to the death of faith, hope, and love. Through God's grace, you can choose life—abundant life—life lived with engagement for God and others.

RELATING TRUTH TO LIFE: YOUR WORSHIPING GRIEF AND GROWTH WORKBOOK

As you read the following worshiping grief and growth exercises, create your own personal workout routine, selecting the *journey* assignments and the *journal* questions that are best for you. In this chapter, I've designed your growth work to help *you* to move from *digging cisterns to worshiping God—engaging with love.* You can want God more than you want relief. You can find God even when you don't find answers. You can walk with God in the dark and have Him as the light of your soul.

I pray that the following exercises will assist you to trace your weaving *journey*—what your path has been like so far and how you can continue to move forward. And I pray that these exercises will help you to develop your weaving *journal*—putting words (whether written or thought) to your growth—grieving with hope.

YOUR WORSHIPING JOURNEY

1. In worshiping, you refuse to turn to false lovers of the soul and you choose to worship God. Where would you rate yourself on a scale of 1-10, with 1 being digging broken cisterns that hold no water and 10 being finding God even when you can't find answers?

2. In past times of suffering, how did you begin to move from false God substitutes to worshiping God—engaging God with love and engaging others with God's love?

3. Satan wants to use suffering to cause you to doubt God and to turn to false idols of the heart. In what ways have you faced such temptation? How are you overcoming them?

4. Facing his suffering, Asaph said, "Whom have I in heaven but you? And earth has nothing I desire besides you" (Psalm 73:25). In what ways are you responding to suffering like Asaph?

5. Find a trusted, safe friend and take the step of sharing with him or her any temptations you are facing to dig cisterns. Also share ways God is giving you the victory by empowering you to worship Him and minister to others.

YOUR WORSHIPING JOURNAL

1. You have two choices in suffering: digging broken cisterns that hold no water, or drinking from God your Spring of Living Water (Jeremiah 2:13). How can you drink from God?

2. What false lovers of the soul and sinful idols of the heart are you tempted to wed yourself to, when you try to face suffering without facing God?

3. In your suffering, what does it look like for you to admit your insufficiency and cling to God? Are you longing for God? Straining to glimpse the face of God?

4. Which do you want more, God or relief?

5. How are you finding God even when you don't find answers?

6. How are you walking with God in the dark and finding Him to be the light of your soul?

7. How are you using your suffering as an opportunity to know God better?

8. How are your problems influencing your relationship to God?

9. Suffering can either shove us far from God or drag us, kicking and screaming, closer to Him. In which direction do you seem headed?

10. Like David, how can your grief create God-thirst? "As the deer pants for streams of water, so my soul pants for you, O God. My soul thirsts for God, for the living God. When can I go and meet with God?" (Psalm 42:1-2).

THE JOURNEY CONTINUES

We've come near the end of our written journey. Of course, your personal journey of grieving and growing will continue.

We'll talk more about where you go from here in the Conclusion—but don't even let the word "conclusion" fool you. No one is saying that your journey has concluded. We'll simply reflect and ponder how your journey thus far can impact your continued walk with God so you can find God's healing for your losses and God's hope for your hurts.

CONCLUSION
The Rest of the Story

———◆———

JESUS PROMISES THAT ONE DAY HE WILL WIPE AWAY ALL PAIN from every loss.

Now, that's the promise you were hoping for!

In Revelation 7, Jesus grants the apostle John a glimpse into the future. The Lamb of God at the center of the universal throne is shepherding God's people; leading them to springs of living water.

THE PROMISE OF A LIFETIME

Reaching those healing, life-giving waters, John gives us the promise of a lifetime. "And God will wipe away every tear from their eyes" (Revelation 7:17).

Just in case it seems beyond belief, in Revelation 21 John repeats and expands Jesus' message of hope. Peering into the new heaven and the new earth, John tells us that God "will wipe every tear from their eyes. There will be no more death or mourning or crying or pain, for the old order of things has passed away" (Revelation 21:4).

We've all heard it so many times that the impact dissipates. Let the reality hit home—go back to the future.

God *is* dwelling with you.

God reaches down to wipe *every* tear from *your* eyes.

God's booming, loving voice *reassures you* that death, separation, suffering, and grieving are all a thing of the past. "My child," He sweetly whispers, "no more mourning, or crying, or pain."

Every mini-casket death-and-separation experience will be swallowed up in victory. Every major-casket death-and-separation experience will be defeated so you can say with the Apostle Paul, "Where, O death, is your sting?" (1 Corinthians 15:55).

READING THE END OF THE STORY

Paul concludes his discussion of our future hope by encouraging us to stand firm, to be unmovable, and to be fully committed to worship and ministry (1 Corinthians 15:58). But in the midst of life's losses, how are we supposed to do that?

When life dashes our dreams and seems to kill our hopes, we must remind ourselves that we've read the end of the story. We need to listen like we would to Paul Harvey's *The Rest of the Story*.

Many sports fans, if they can't watch the big game live, tape it. Then they swear all their friends to secrecy. "Don't you dare spoil it for me! Don't tell me who won. I want to watch it and enjoy the thrill of the whole game without knowing the end."

I guess I'm odd. When I can't watch the big game live, I tape it, but I watch the end first! I'm a major fan of the Chicago Bulls. Back when Michael Jordan was leading them to six NBA titles, I taped one of the championship games between the Bulls and the Phoenix Suns. First, I watched the end. The Bulls won! Then I rewound the tape and watched the entire game. When the Bulls were behind by 17 points, I never panicked. I never threw bricks at the TV.

Normally I would have left the room if they were behind by that much. I would have told my son to call me only if the Bulls tied the game. I couldn't take watching them struggle. But not this time. I knew the end of the story. So I could handle the ups and downs of the game, knowing the grand result.

Whether or not you agree with my sports-watching philosophy, you can see the benefits we gain from knowing the end of God's story—the end of *our* story. We can survive life's losses and we can even thrive through God's hope when we remember the end of the story.

We've read the end of the story. And we win! God wins!

We've read the end of the story.
And we win! God wins!

In the end:
Healing triumphs over losses.
Hope triumphs over hurt.
Grace triumphs over works.
Faith triumphs over doubt.
Hope triumphs over despair.
Love triumphs over separation.
Life triumphs over death.
Good triumphs over evil.
God triumphs over the devil.

THE QUILTING OF YOUR LIFE

We began with present reality: "I have told you these things, so that in me you may have peace. In this world you will have *trouble*" (John 16:33).

We conclude with future reality: God "will wipe every tear from their eyes. There will be no more death or mourning or crying or pain, for the old order of things has passed away" (Revelation 21:4).

We live between these two worlds. We journey aware of both realities.

It bears repeating that our journey is not a straight line. We don't move in an easy, linear direction from "stage" one to "stage" eight. Life is far too messy for that.

More than that, the human soul is far too complex for us to imagine that a "few easy steps" move us all the way from denial to worship. While we might try to quantify a "grief process," the suffering soul can't be computed, measured, or calculated.

Grief is never a nice, neat package. Finding hope when you're hurting follows no outline. Whatever "process" there is, it is uniquely personal. And that process is more like two stages forward and one stage back. Perhaps even more realistically, you may find yourself in several stages at any one time.

I've mapped out a "pattern" from my understanding of Scripture, my personal engagement with suffering, and my pastoral care and counseling with hurting spiritual friends. As you apply this pattern to your life, it becomes your own personal quilt, woven together day-by-day by you, and God's people, and God's Spirit.

Looking at any one section of your life quilt, you might see only seemingly random threads. The colors and contours may not seem to make any sense whatsoever. But because God's Word is sufficient and relevant, you can be confident that through Christ you are weaving a beautiful tapestry.

Knowing the rest of the story
provides rest for the soul.

REST FOR YOUR SOUL

I know how hard hopeful trust can be. I've suffered great losses, too. The ache at times has seemed unbearable, unmanageable. Hope has seemed unobtainable. Rest unimaginable. Healing impossible.

However, with God, all things are possible. That's no cliché. That's inspired truth. Hope is supernatural. Healing is possible. Knowing the rest of the story provides rest for the soul.

So, please, don't give up. Keep facing life face-to-face with God.

Healing is coming. Hope is on the horizon.

New life is in the air. Resurrection power is at work.

Jesus is on the move. He's speaking to you now. "Come to me, all you who are weary and burdened, and I will give you rest" (Matthew 11:28).

In Christ, find rest for your soul. Find healing for life's losses. Find hope when you're hurting.

ENDNOTES

INTRODUCTION
[1]Lake, *Clinical Theology*, 58.
[2]Packer, *Rediscovering Holiness*, 249, 254, emphasis added.
[3]Lake, 97.
[4]Waite, *Taken on Trust*, 37.
[5]Hurnard, *Hinds' Feet on High Places*, 65-66.
[6]Ibid., 66.
[7]Ibid.

CHAPTER ONE
[1]Wangerin, *Mourning into Dancing*, 26.
[2]Ibid., 76.
[3]Kreeft, *Making Sense Out of Suffering*, 78.
[4]Kubler-Ross, *On Death and Dying*, throughout.
[5]Willard, *The Spirit of the Disciplines*, 45.

CHAPTER FOUR
[1]Lake, 24-25, emphasis added.
[2]Lewis, *The Problem of Pain*, 83.

CHAPTER EIGHT
[1]Luther, *Luther's Works*, Vol. 42, 24.
[2]Strohl, "Luther's Fourteen Consolations," 179.
[3]Luther, 154.
[4]Ibid., 165.

BIBLIOGRAPHY

Adams, Jay. *More Than Redemption: A Theology of Christian Counseling*. Grand Rapids: Zondervan, 1979.

Aden, L. "Comfort/Sustaining." Pages 193-195 in *The Dictionary of Pastoral Care and Counseling*. Edited by R. J. Hunter. Nashville: Abingdon Press, 1990.

Allender, Dan, and Tremper Longman. *The Cry of the Soul: How Our Emotions Reveal Our Deepest Questions About God*. Colorado Springs: NavPress, 1994.

Graham, L. K. "Healing." Pages 497-501 in *The Dictionary of Pastoral Care and Counseling*. Edited by R. J. Hunter. Nashville: Abingdon Press, 1990.

Hsu, Albert. *Grieving a Suicide: A Loved One's Search for Comfort, Answers, and Hope*. Downers Grove, Ill.: InterVarsity Press, 2002.

Hurnard, Hannah. *Hinds' Feet on High Places*. Wheaton: Tyndale House, 1975.

Kellemen, Robert. *Soul Physicians: A Theology of Soul Care and Spiritual Direction*. Third revised edition. Winona Lake, Ind.: BMH Books, 2007.

_____ *Spiritual Friends: A Methodology of Soul Care and Spiritual Direction*. Revised third edition. Winona Lake, Ind.: BMH Books, 2007.

_____ "Spiritual Care in Historical Perspective: Martin Luther as a Case Study in Christian Sustaining, Healing, Reconciling, and Guiding." Ph.D. Dissertation, Kent State University, 1997.

Kellemen, Robert, and Karole Edwards. *Beyond the Suffering: Embracing the Legacy of African American Soul Care and Spiritual Direction*. Grand Rapids: Baker Books, 2007.

Kellemen, Robert, and Susan Ellis. *Sacred Friendships: Celebrating the Legacy of Women Heroes of the Faith*. Winona Lake, Ind.: BMH Books, 2009.

Kreeft, Peter. *Making Sense Out of Suffering*. Ann Arbor, Mich.: Servant Books, 1986.

Kubler-Ross, Elisabeth. *On Death and Dying*. New York: MacMillan, 1969.

Kubler-Ross, Elisabeth, and David Kessler. *On Grief and Grieving: Finding the Meaning of Grief through the Five Stages of Loss*. New York: Scribner, 2007.

Lake, Frank. *Clinical Theology*. London: Darton, Longman & Todd, 1966.

Lewis, C. S. *The Problem of Pain*. Reprint. New York: Simon & Schuster, 1996.

Luther, Martin. *Devotional Writings I*. Vol. 42 of *Luther's Works*. Edited and translated by M. O. Dietrich. Philadelphia: Fortress Press, 1969.

Packer, J. I. *Rediscovering Holiness*. Ann Arbor, Mich.: Servant Publications, 1992.

Strohl, J. E. "Luther's Fourteen Consolations." *Lutheran Quarterly* 3 (1989): 169-182.

Tiegreen, Chris. *Why a Suffering World Makes Sense*. Grand Rapids: Baker Books, 2006.

Waite, Terry. *Taken on Trust*. New York: Harcourt, Brace & Co., 1993.

Wangerin, Walter. *Mourning into Dancing*. Grand Rapids: Zondervan, 1992.

Welch, Edward. *Depression: A Stubborn Darkness—Light for the Path*. Second printing. Winston-Salem, N.C.: Punch Press, 2004.

Westbert, Granger. *Good Grief*. Thirty-fifth anniversary edition. Minneapolis: Fortress Press, 1997.

Willard, Dallas. *The Spirit of the Disciplines: Understanding How God Changes Lives*. San Francisco: Harper, 1991.

Zonnebelt-Smeenge, Susan, and Robert De Vries. *Getting to the Other Side of Grief: Overcoming the Loss of a Spouse*. Grand Rapids: Baker Books, 1998.

RESOURCES FOR YOUR JOURNEY
from Dr. Kellemen and RPM Ministries

Bob Kellemen, Ph.D., LCPC, doesn't want his ministry to you to stop when you've turned the last page of this book.

Contact him at *rpm.ministries@gmail.com* if you'd like him to minister to your church or para-church group on *God's Healing for Life's Losses* (creative, powerful, interactive, healing half-day or all-day seminars).

Be fed daily at his Changeless Truth for Changing Times blog: *www.rpmministries.org*.

Visit his RPM Ministries website for scores of free resources, inspiring quotes, books, and e-books: *www.rpmministries.org*.

Be equipped to change lives with Christ's changeless truth through "Doc. K's" books on Christ-centered, comprehensive, compassionate, and culturally-informed biblical counseling and spiritual formation. Order from *www.bmhbooks.com* or from *www.rpmministries.org*.

- *Soul Physicians: A Theology of Soul Care and Spiritual Direction*
- *Spiritual Friends: A Methodology of Soul Care and Spiritual Direction*
- *Sacred Friendships: Celebrating the Legacy of Women Heroes of the Faith*
- *Beyond the Suffering: Embracing the Legacy of African American Soul Care and Spiritual Direction*

Dr. Robert W. Kellemen served for more than a dozen years as chairman of the Master of Arts in Christian Counseling and Discipleship Department at Capital Bible Seminary. He is now Professor-at-Large in that Department. In his three pastoral ministries, Bob has ministered to hundreds of grieving parishioners. In his role as Founder and CEO of RPM Ministries (*www.rpmminstries.org*) Bob is known for his Christ-centered, comprehensive, compassionate, and culturally-informed approach to equipping God's people to use God's Word in their personal ministry. Bob is also the Executive Director of the Association of Biblical Counselors' Center for Church Equipping.